A Masterwork
of Doubting-Belief

A Masterwork
of Doubting-Belief

R. S. Thomas and His Poetry

JOHN G. MCELLHENNEY

WIPF & STOCK · Eugene, Oregon

A MASTERWORK OF DOUBTING-BELIEF
R. S. Thomas and His Poetry

Wipf & Stock
An imprint of Wipf and Stock Publishers
199 W. 8th Ave., Suite 3
Eugene, OR 97401

www.wipfandstock.com

ISBN 13: 978-1-61097-310-6

Manufactured in the U.S.A.

For

Nancy

and

Peter

Contents

Acknowledgments

This book owes its existence to Nancy, my wife.

On Sunday, August 9, 1992, several days before I was to meet R. S. Thomas for the first time, I checked in at the Maybank Hotel in Aberdyfi, Wales, and immediately called Nancy back home in West Chester, Pennsylvania. She told me her mother had died the day before. During the closing weeks of Mother Wolf's life, Nancy made a number of brave and loving decisions. Now she made one more: She allowed me to remain in Wales and complete my plans for seeing Thomas. When he and I met on August 12, this book became a possibility; twenty years later, a reality. So it would not exist if it were not for the strength and kindness of Nancy.

It would not have its shape without Peter, our writer son. Peter was with Nancy at the time his grandmother died, and has been with me every keystroke of this book's way. He focused my thinking and channeled my writing. When the end was in sight, his proposal for combining two chapters and Peggy Rosenthal's recommended changes provided the thrust I needed to finish my work.

Robert Feaster critiqued my manuscript at several stages and encouraged me to keep at it. Andrew Scrimgeour brought the project to realization by finding a publisher. Jay Brenneman, William Lentz, and William McGill, in addition to Peggy Rosenthal, served as readers.

Over the past forty years, my thinking about Thomas's poetry has been tested in conversations with Charles Bartolett, Dale Owens, Dennis Williams, Robert Wright, and Charles Yrigoyen Jr. The people of four congregations responded to my Thomas interpretations: the Ardmore, West Chester, and Wayne United

Methodist churches and St. Peter's Episcopal Church in the Great Valley. At the invitation of Elizabeth (Sue) Moore, Prior General of the Order of Saint Luke, I led discussions of Thomas's poems at two retreats of the New Jersey Chapter of the Order. And students in the seminary classes I taught were asked to read and comment on Thomas's "Hidden God" poetry.

Four couples—Louise and Charles Bartolett, Patricia and Dale Owens, Marianne and Robert Wright, Jeanette and Charles Yrigoyen Jr.—accompanied Nancy and me when we visited Thomas at Aberdyfi, Wales, in 1993. Their memories of our talks with Thomas enrich chapter 4.

Gwydion Thomas and Kunjana Thomas were most generous in granting permission to quote from the works of R. S. Thomas—to them a closing word of grateful indebtedness.

Introduction

THE POET R. S. Thomas and many of his poems provide a model for doubting-believers, persons who simultaneously believe and doubt, like the father in the Bible whose son suffered from epileptic seizures. When Jesus challenged him to believe that his little boy could be convulsion-free, he replied, "I believe; help my unbelief!"[1]

R. S. Thomas always believed. His mother, who grew up in the home of an Anglican vicar, introduced her son to belief in God, taking him with her to church. His intellectual understanding of God was shaped by his formal theological studies; more, however, by his work as a parish priest and by his own program of reading.

Often Thomas's experiences of God, as opposed to his thinking about God, took place not in church buildings but outdoors, in the sanctuary of nature. Indeed, his natural habitat was the tip of a peninsula, a place where land, sea, and sky edge into one another; a place where *infinity* is an experience, not a concept. There he waited for migratory birds to appear. There he waited for experiences of God's elusive, migratory, presence.

Thomas's doubts may be traced to a number of sources. One is that as a poet he was responsive to the imperatives of his muse. And since a poet's muse acknowledges no orthodoxy, subscribes to no creed, the muse may nudge the poet to express doubts that other believers conceal, even from themselves.

Another source of Thomas's doubt is that he knew the Bible too well not to be appalled by the bloodthirsty God depicted in some of its passages. He was too familiar with the holocausts of

---

1. Mark 9:24.

history not to wonder if God is just and good. His grasp of science was too complete not to realize that scientists do not need God as a hypothesis.

The tension between believing and doubting is just one of the contradictions in Thomas's life, one of his hyphenated identities. He refused to have electric lights outside his cottage, which stood in the shadow of a nuclear power plant, because they blurred his view of the stars. Inside, there was a real wood fire in the grate, electric lights that drew energy from the nuclear plant, and a poet who was active in the movement for a nuclear free Wales. He campaigned for using Welsh on road signs and in official documents. Yet he wrote his poems in English, signed contracts with London publishers, and depended upon English reviewers to build an audience of avid readers.

When a camera was present, Thomas often did his best to look like one of the carved stone heads of Easter Island. To put off English reporters, he replied to their questions in Welsh. People who saw only the public side of Thomas thought of him as reclusive, cantankerous, or worse. In private, however, he was a personable, thoughtful man, who had a keen sense of humor. For me, he is a man who wrote caring, if sometimes cranky letters, and was willing to let me visit him more than once.

These inconsistencies serve as a reminder that poets, for all their gifts of insight and expression, are human like us. But the tensions between incompatibles in Thomas's life are more than mere examples of his humanness. They may be understood as irritants that released his poetic gifts the way grains of sand irritate oysters.

The tension between belief and doubt—between Thomas's uneroding belief in the existence of God and his ongoing doubts about the presence, justice, and goodness of God—played a key part in triggering the composition of the poems that make Thomas one of the greatest poets of the God of the Bible, the God Who Hides, the God who identifies himself enigmatically as *I Am Who I Am.*[2]

---

2. Exod 3:14.

The tug, almost of war, between doubt and belief is not just an irritant that releases poetic creativity. It is, as Thomas well understood, a necessary component of belief. For belief needs doubt to temper it, to make it more flexible, to enable it to bear up under Shakespeare's "whips and scorns of time." Many believers deny their doubts, using noisy assertions of rock-solid faith to drown out the insistent voices of uncertainty. Thomas, on the other hand, knew that when persons hide their religious uncertainties, they open themselves to spiritual decay. For concealed doubts are like untreated diseases: They fester and sap strength until, when a major blow comes, the person has no spiritual resources left to withstand it.

Thomas revealed his doubts, poured them into poems that question God's justice and goodness; poems that deal with the poet's experiences of divine remoteness. The overall effect of these poems is not negative, however. For when we put our doubts into words, they stop haunting us. Like heat tempering steel, doubts admitted make belief flexible, better able to resist Hamlet's "slings and arrows of outrageous fortune."

In addition to understanding that belief needs doubt to temper it, Thomas recognized that doubting-belief correlates with the nature of God's self-revelation. God chooses to hide from the human mind, to resist even the most sophisticated efforts to prove the divine existence. At the same time, God chooses to be present occasionally to the intuitions of the heart, to be more real than any proof put forth by science or philosophy. Therefore belief will always be hyphenated with doubt.

From R. S. Thomas to R. S. to Ronald

The genesis of my interest in Thomas was nearly forty years ago, when I read an article about his poetry in the *Saturday Review*. I ordered the reviewed book, a volume of selected poems, and before long was buying Thomas's new works and asking secondhand book dealers to find copies of his older ones. Later, I initiated a personal relationship with Thomas, first by correspondence, then by visits. The progressive stages of that relationship are marked by the changing way he signed his letters: *R. S. Thomas*, then *R. S.*, finally *Ronald*.

This book, too, develops in stages, moving along a line that is both chronological and thematic. The chronology begins at Thomas's birth in 1913 and ends with his death in 2000. The thematic movement begins with a chapter that presents three of the hyphenated identities that shaped Thomas's life and spurred his poetry: Anglo-Cymric, land-sea-sky, and poet-priest. Chapter 2 deals with Thomas as a doubting-believer. It is followed by three chapters that report on my trips to Wales in 1992, 1993, and 1994. Visiting with Thomas, I discovered his personable, even funny private side, in contrast with the public view of him as stone-faced and cranky. Chapters 6 and 7 draw on the interview I conducted with Thomas during my 1994 visit, which added significant information to what I already knew about his theology and the writers who influenced him. Chapter 8, titled "My Health Seems to Have Completely Broken Down," uses his letters to cover his life from my 1994 visit to his death.

1

Hyphenated Man

A DRIVE WITH MY parents into the forested hills of Union County, Pennsylvania, to cut a Christmas tree introduced me to the way that irreconcilable events are often indissolubly wed.

I was seven years old. We had gone to church, eaten lunch, taken a ride, picked a tree, returned to town, and parked in front of our house, when Uncle Harry came dashing across the street, calling, "Have you heard? The Japanese attacked Pearl Harbor!" The only link between those irreconcilables, a tree of peace and an act of war, was a common date, December 7, 1941, which hyphenated them in my memory.

That boyhood experience of contradictory realities connected by a hyphen began preparing me to understand R. S. Thomas as a hyphenated man. Thomas was a bundle of irreconcilable but linked identities. He tied together his English and Welsh heritages. He was a man of land-sea-sky, who felt dislocated when he was out of sight of any one of those three. And he experienced twin, perhaps mutually repelling, callings: priest and poet. Each of these hyphenated identities persisted throughout his long life, but this chapter highlights them in relation to particular times, places, and experiences.

Anglo-Cymric—1913–1932— Cardiff, Several Seaports, Holyhead

Anglo refers to the English part of Thomas's identity; *Cymric* is an adjective derived from *Cymru*, the Welsh word for Wales.

Thomas was born, in 1913, in Cardiff, the capital of Wales, but his birth language was English. His name, Ronald Stuart Thomas, proclaims his hyphenated identity: *Thomas* is a quintessentially Welsh surname; *Ronald Stuart* are English given names. His ancestors were Welsh on both sides, but his father did not speak Welsh, at least not at home; and his mother's only language was English.

During the First World War, because Thomas's father was an officer in the merchant navy, he and his mother moved from seaport to seaport. Usually these were English ports, such as London, Liverpool, and Goole, a city on the east coast of England, from which the elder Thomas sailed to Antwerp.

In 1919, the year of the Treaty of Versailles, the Thomas family settled in Holyhead, a seaport in northwestern Wales, where English men and women coming by train from London picked up the ferry to Dublin on which Thomas's father was a second mate. Holyhead, then, was as much, if not more, English than Welsh. Thomas's schooling was in English; he and his mother attended English-language worship services of the Church in Wales, a province of the Anglican Communion.

Throughout his life, the more Thomas tugged himself towards his Welsh heritage, the more his Englishness resisted. His Welsh *Thomas* was always at loggerheads with his English *Ronald*. He chose to be a poet in a land of legendary bards, yet was forced to write his poems in the language of the suppressors of the bardic tradition. He developed a passionate attachment to his Welsh heritage, to the history and culture of Wales. He lived, however, among Welsh men and women who were content, even eager, to submit to English culture. The bitterness produced by this tension emerges in his poem "Reservoirs."

"Reservoirs" alludes to the death, in 1965, of the village of Capel Celyn in North Wales. English authorities decided that the English city of Liverpool's need for water outweighed the right of the Welsh village to live. So they dammed the river Tryweryn to create a reservoir, which became a tomb for Capel Celyn's chapel, school, post office, farms, and twelve homes.

The serene mask worn by Llyn Celyn and other tomb-lakes revolted Thomas:

> There are places in Wales I don't go:
> Reservoirs that are the subconscious
> Of a people, troubled far down
> With gravestones, chapels, villages even;
> The serenity of their expression
> Revolts me, it is a pose
> For strangers, a watercolour's appeal
> To the mass, instead of the poem's
> Harsher conditions. There are the hills,
> Too; gardens gone under the scum
> Of the forests; and the smashed faces
> Of the farms with the stone trickle
> Of their tears down the hills' side.
>
> Where can I go, then, from the smell
> Of decay, from the putrefying of a dead
> Nation? I have walked the shore
> For an hour and seen the English
> Scavenging among the remains
> Of our culture, covering the sand
> Like the tide and, with the roughness
> Of the tide, elbowing our language
> Into the grave that we have dug for it.[1]

Thomas's description of the complicity of the Welsh in the English suppression of the Welsh language reminds me of things he said in letters to me. When I was planning the details of my first meeting with Thomas, I wrote and told him that I had reserved a room at Carreg Plas, a country guesthouse not far from the cottage where he was living in retirement. Responding, he said

1. Thomas, *Collected Poems 1945–1990*, 194; "Reservoirs" ("There are places in Wales I don't go"). The footnotes identify Thomas's titled poems by their title, followed by their first line in parentheses. His untitled poems are identified by their first line.

he had no knowledge of Carreg Plas; that it was, no doubt, run by English people who were happy to be part of the United Kingdom, the English-concocted union of England, Wales, and Scotland. My next letter asked him to suggest a Welsh-owned guesthouse. No, he answered; best to stick with English-owned and -operated Carreg Plas. Centuries of being subjected to English domination had bred a "serf mentality" in Welsh men and women. So they preferred "to skivvy for the English rather than risk running things themselves."

That was my personal introduction to Thomas's penchant for taking digs at Welsh people who kowtow to the English, and at English people who live in Wales but make no effort to baptize themselves in Welshness. He was, of course, taking digs at his own hyphenated identity, at his contradictory English and Welsh heritages. He was skewering his desire to be *the* poetic celebrant of Wales and Welshness, while being obliged, because his birth language was English, to celebrate his Welsh patrimony in the tongue of its English dispossessors.

Land-Sea-Sky—1932–1942—
Bangor, Llandaff, Chirk, and Hanmer

To be himself, to fulfill his nature, Thomas needed to be able to walk out from his house into open countryside, to stroll through meadows and moors, to have hills and mountains to look up to. He needed an expansive sky, with scudding clouds by day; with stars at night not dimmed by artificial light floating up from cities and towns. Especially he needed to be able to see the sea, hear its murmur or its roar, taste its salt in the air, wait and watch for its migratory birds.

Thomas grew up, as we have seen, in Holyhead, which, he said, stands for "the sea." Holyhead is located on an island separated by a narrow strip of water from Anglesey, which is an island cut off by the Menai Strait from the mainland of Wales. "The sea," Thomas remembered, became part of his life as a child, "its noise, its smell, its ferocity on windy days. It was to be seen from his bedroom."[2]

When he left Holyhead, in 1932, to enter the University of North Wales in Bangor, Thomas continued to live close to the sea, for Bangor stands at the junction of the Menai Strait and Conwy Bay. Speaking about a student, who may have been himself, he recalled that when you took a girl out rowing, you'd often forget that the row home was against the tide.

While living in Bangor, the mountains of Snowdonia entered Thomas's life. Given the choice between a library tome and a mountain trek, he often chose the latter. He did "only // enough work to enable / him to answer set / questions" in the classic literature of Greece and Rome, his chosen field of study to prepare him for ordination as a priest of the Church in Wales:

> He rationed his intake
> of knowledge. On fine days
> with the mountain leaning
> over him to whisper
>
> there were other picnics
> beside the musty sandwiches
> in the library. . . .[3]

By the time, 1935, that Thomas received his university degree, he was definitively a land-sea-sky man. This identity was challenged when he moved to Llandaff, a suburb of Cardiff, to continue his studies for the priesthood at St. Michael's Theological College. Although Cardiff is located where the Mouth of the Severn opens into the Bristol Channel, its relationship to water is commercial, bustling, noisy; not at all conducive to birdwatching, to quietly waiting for a poem to drift into sight.

Thomas experienced disarrangement at Llandaff. He couldn't see and hear the sea from his college room, and moors and mountains were a train ride away. So when he heard that a vicar was looking for a curate, he applied for the position. The bishop agreed

2. Thomas, *Autobiographies*, 30.
3. Thomas, *Collected Later Poems 1988–2000*, 18; "He rationed his intake."

to ordain him deacon after just one year of St. Michael's standard two-year theological program. This made it possible for Thomas to move to Chirk, a town on the eastern side of Wales, not far from the English border. The next year, 1937, he received priest's ordination.

Thomas's escape from Llandaff locked him in a new prison, an industrialized area far from mountains and the sea. He endured, pined, did his parish work, and met Elsie (Elsi in Welsh) Eldridge. They married in 1940, and, because the vicar of Chirk did not want a married curate, he accepted a curacy even farther away from the Welsh mountains and the sea, in Hanmer, which is a sort of finger of dull countryside sticking into the back of England—a place where the sun "cracks the cheeks / Of the gaunt sky perhaps once in a week."[4]

Hanmer was on the Luftwaffe's path for its nightly assaults on Liverpool's docks.

> Skies were red where no
> sun had ever risen
> or set. He learned fear,
> the instinctive fear
>
> of the animal that finds
> the foliage about its den
> disarranged . . . .[5]

Fear for his wife's life and his own—stray bombs dropped close to where they lived—and a general sense of disarrangement led Thomas to seek a parish deeper in the heart of Wales, closer to the mountains, closer to the sea. He found that parish, St. Michael and All Angels, Manafon, in 1942. Here there were moors and hills for long afternoon walks. Higher mountains, even legend-embroidered Cader Idris, were visible. But the sea was much too far away, especially during the years of wartime petrol rationing. So Thomas

---

4. Thomas, *Collected Poems* 1945–1990, 4; "A Peasant" ("Iago Prytherch his name, though, be it allowed").

5. Thomas, *Collected Later Poems* 1988–2000, 20; "In the country house."

remained dislocated: He could be a land-sky man at Manafon, but not a man of the sea.

Thomas's identity as a land-sea-sky man existed in tension with any place he lived that cut him off from that vitalizing triad. His natural habitat was a place where the landscape was open but bordered by hills, if not mountains; where the sky was large by day and star-filled at night; where the sea's waving could be seen, its roar heard, its salty air tasted. Bangor, which he left in 1935, was the last location that offered Thomas that life-sustaining combination until he moved, in 1967, to Aberdovey, which is located, in his words, at the tip of "a bough / of country that is suspended / between sky and sea."[6] There, truly located at last, Thomas became the master poet of doubting-belief in God.

For now, we'll return to Thomas's Manafon years, to the period when his identity as a poet-priest was established.

POET-PRIEST—1942–1954—MANAFON

Some houses, a school, a shop, the Church of St. Michael and All Angels, and a pub, all strung out along a road that meanders beside the river Rhiw in the hill country of Central Wales—that's Manafon. The slopes of the hills are dotted with farms; higher up are sheep pastures.

A few miles west of Manafon, along a one-track road, is Adfa; just a chapel and several houses at the edge of extensive white space on the map. Walking out from Adfa, Thomas could savor his aloneness under a cloud-pocked sky, against the backdrop of mountains to the west.

Back in Manafon, he turned down a lane to the white house, the rectory, in which he and Elsi and, later, their son, Gwydion, lived from 1942 to 1954. "Coming home," he wrote,

---

6. Thomas, *Collected Poems 1945–1990*, 503; "Retirement" ("I have crawled out at last").

> was to that:
> The white house in the cool grass
> Membraned with shadow, the bright stretch
> Of stream that was its looking-glass;
>
> And smoke growing above the roof
> To a tall tree among whose boughs
> The first stars renewed their theme
> Of time and death and a man's vows.[7]

The obvious vows are the ones Thomas took when he and Elsi married. But the white house was a rectory, so there were also the vows he took when a bishop ordained him to the priesthood. Finally, Thomas had vowed to himself to be a poet. The second and third of his vows constituted his public identity, that of poet-priest.

Manafon was a good place for Thomas the poet to live. There were moors in the Manafon area that Thomas could enter as he entered a church, "on soft foot, / Breath held like a cap in the hand. / It was quiet."[8] Beyond the moors were mountains, to which Thomas, the worshiper in God's outdoors sanctuary, could lift up his eyes. But back in his parish, on the hill farms around Manafon, there were people who reeked of the barnyard; men and women whose "clothes, sour with years of sweat / And animal contact, shock the refined, / But affected, sense with their stark naturalness."[9]

Thomas arrived in Manafon as "a little bourgeois, well-bred, with the mark of the church and library upon me."[10] His uppity nose twitched at odors that town churches and university libraries had not accustomed him to. But the manure-laced aromas of Manafon were just the inhaled aspect of what shocked him. Much more distressing to Thomas the priest was the fact that he was serving in an area "where flesh meets spirit / Only on Sundays and the days between / Are mortgaged to the grasping soil."[11]

7. Ibid., 64; "The Return" ("Coming home was to that").

8. Ibid., 166; "The Moor" ("It was like a church to me").

9. Ibid., 4; "A Peasant" ("Iago Prytherch his name, though, be it allowed").

10. Thomas, *Autobiographies*, 11.

11. Thomas, *Collected Poems* 1945–1990, 42; "The Minister" ("In the hill country at the moor's edge").

The sensibilities and perceptions that make a person a poet had never developed in Thomas's Manafon parishioners, who had been taught by their soil how to be grasping, tight-fisted, calculating. They were content to let their parish priest spend weekday mornings in his study, his afternoons walking the hillsides and moors, his evenings visiting from cottage to cottage. They expected him, of course, to lead the prayerbook services on Sundays, preach, celebrate the Eucharist; to baptize, officiate at marriages, bury the dead. But his satisfying of those expectations did not overcome a certain tenseness between the parishioners and their poet-priest. "Was it," Thomas asks in his autobiography,

> because of the hardness of the people and their work, or because of some nicety in himself, that the tension arose that was to be a part of his spiritual and literary problems for so many years? At the time he was too young and too inexperienced to know that tension is an irremovable part of art.[12]

The tension between Thomas and his parishioners, between spirit and flesh, between refined and unrefined, between library and pigsty, helped release the flow of his poetry. This tension is one of the themes in a poem about a priest and his parishioners that the tension itself helped to create:

> The priest picks his way
> Through the parish. Eyes watch him
> From windows, from the farms;
> Hearts wanting him to come near.
> The flesh rejects him.
>
> Women, pouring from the black kettle,
> Stir up the whirling tea-grounds
> Of their thoughts; offer him a dark
> Filling in their smiling sandwich.
>
> Priests have a long way to go.
> The people wait for them to come
> To them over the broken glass
> Of their vows, making them pay
> With the sweat's coinage for their correction.

12. Thomas, *Autobiographies*, 52.

> He goes up a green lane
> Through growing birches; lambs cushion
> His vision. He comes slowly down
> In the dark, feeling the cross warp
> In his hands; hanging on it his thought's icicles.
>
> 'Crippled soul,' do you say? looking at him
> From the mind's height; 'limping through life
> On his prayers. There are other people
> In the world, sitting at table
> Contented, though the broken body
> And the shed blood are not on the menu.'
>
> 'Let it be so,' I say. 'Amen and amen.'[13]

Only a parish priest who was also a master poet could have written that poem, a poem that perfectly captures the experience of every parish minister. Certainly I recall the smiling woman who said, "That was a wonderful sermon, pastor!" The dark filling? She slept during the sermon, and her breath had been distilled.

INSPIRATION VERSUS PERSPIRATION

A subsidiary but essential tension within the poet side of the poet-priest hyphenation is the tension between the mysterious flutter that alerts poets to the presence of their muse and the hard, hard work that goes into getting a poem down on paper. Thomas en-fleshes this hyphenation of inspiration and perspiration in two old poets talking over their pints of beer.

I can see those old poets because I can see my first lunch with Thomas. We were seated across from each other at a narrow table in a country inn; our drink was Rhine wine, not beer. There were no other diners that August Wednesday afternoon, so the room was not noisy, not "glib with prose." Thomas pressed his palms into his somewhat sunken cheeks, rested his elbows on the table, and talked about poetry.

13. Thomas, *Collected Poems* 1945–1990, 196; "The Priest" ("The priest picks his way").

'Listen, now, verse should be as natural
As the small tuber that feeds on muck
And grows slowly from obtuse soil
To the white flower of immortal beauty.'

'Natural, hell! What was it Chaucer
Said once about the long toil
That goes like blood to the poem's making?
Leave it to nature and the verse sprawls,
Limp as bindweed, if it break at all
Life's iron crust. Man, you must sweat
And rhyme your guts taut, if you'd build
Your verse a ladder.'
                              'You speak as though
No sunlight ever surprised the mind
Groping on its cloudy path.'

'Sunlight's a thing that needs a window
Before it enter a dark room.
Window's don't happen.'
                              So two old poets,
Hunched at their beer in the low haze
Of an inn parlour, while the talk ran
Noisily by them, glib with prose.[14]

Thomas's Hyphenated Identities Hurt Him into Poetry

W. H. Auden asserted that "mad Ireland hurt" W. B. Yeats "into poetry."[15] I interpret that as a declaration that there was a tension in Yeats's relationship to his native land that jarred loose his talent for writing poems. It was in exile that Dante imagined his *Divine Comedy*. Beethoven was too deaf to hear some of his most sublime music. So perhaps it is when we are tense with worry, uncertainty, fear; when we are torn nearly in two by competing identities, that

14. Ibid., 86; "Poetry for Supper" ("Listen, now, verse should be as natural").
15. Auden, *Selected Poems*, 89; "In Memory of W. B. Yeats."

an opening appears in us, through which our muse enters with a nudge or a wallop of inspiration.

In this chapter, we reviewed a number of the hyphenated identities that hurt Thomas into poetry: Anglo-Cymric, land-sea-sky, poet-priest. Two more major hyphenations remain to be explored. The first, Thomas as a doubting-believer, is the theme of the next chapter.

The final tension is that between Thomas's two faces. To the world at large, Thomas was a stone-faced crank, a recluse, a man who responded in Welsh to impertinent English questioners. The man I learned to know could break into a smile, enjoy table talk, savor ice cream, exhibit impish wit. This personable Thomas, accompanied by the stony one, has been with us already, but he will fully appear in chapter 3 and stay with us as I describe my visits in 1992, 1993, and 1994, and our correspondence from 1991 until his death in 2000.

2

Doubting-Believer

THOMAS TOLD ME HE always believed in God. This belief united him with the vast majority of men and women over the past fifty thousand years, who have found it impossible to accept the idea that everything that *is* came from *nothing*. Not all believers, of course, use God or Allah or Brahma or any of a host of other deity words in the world's Babel of languages. Some speak of a higher power or powers. Some simply declare their openness to the possibility of a realm beyond the one appropriated by our five senses and analyzed by our rational powers.

For Thomas, God is the Ground of Being, to use theologian Paul Tillich's name for the depth dimension of all that is; the Mystery at the core of existence. In, with, and under all the things that *are*, God *is*. God is the atmosphere in which such things as polonium, persimmons, pollock, and persons exist.

Thomas did not very often experience the presence of the Ground of Being, but when he did, if was as if his whole being overflowed with God "as a chalice would / with the sea."[1] No matter how seldom Thomas felt God's presence, his practice of religion never flagged. He practiced it privately, kneeling in prayer, whether by the side of his bed or in centuries-old houses of worship. As a priest, Thomas practiced his religion publicly, reading

1. Thomas, *Collected Poems* 1945–1990, 283; "Suddenly" ("As I had always known").

the prayerbook services, delivering sermons, and celebrating the Eucharist.

Thomas's theology, whether he was aware of it or not, centered on a correlation between the way God reveals and conceals the divine self and the doubting-belief of persons of faith. Because God withholds self-revelation to human intelligence, doubting God is possible; because God grants self-revelation to human intuition, belief in God is possible. The God who is unavailable to cognition elicits out doubt; the God who is available to perception elicits our belief. Doubting-belief, then, is not the fallback position of weak believers. It is the response to God that correlates with the God who is absent to our intellect but occasionally present to our intuition.

In a poem published after his death, Thomas refers to "transmissions" from this God:

> . . . transmissions
> of a being that has nothing
> to apprise me of but its presence.[2]

God transmits messages to us that assure us that God *is*, that God is with us. But these messages do not supply us with God-information; do not spell out the nature of God.

For Thomas, God is defined simply as Being. Yet in the quote above, he uses "a being," which, perhaps, the constraints of writing poetry forced him to do. But when he was not constricted by syllable count and rhythm, he insisted that God is Being, not a being; not a supernatural being in the midst of a host of natural beings, but Being—the immaterial Reality that underlies all material realities.

The existence of this Ground of Being cannot be established by the mind; cannot be proved by the arguments of philosophers, cannot be demonstrated by the methods of scientists. It is possible, however, to infer God's existence. Happenings may be noticed that suggest the activity of a Power greater than the powers identified by philosophy and science. Thomas writes:

2. Thomas, *Collected Later Poems* 1988–2000, 351; "Temptation" ("Not a door between us, nor a gate").

Never known as anything
but an absence, I dare not name him
as God. Yet the adjustments
are made. There is an unseen
power, whose sphere is the cell
and the electron. We never catch
him at work, but can only say,
coming suddenly upon an amendment,
that here he has been.[3]

While the mind never tracks God on its radar screen, the heart senses "that here he has been."

We *know* God as an absence; we *intuit* God as a presence. Thomas valued ratiocination, the wondrous workings of Hercule Poirot's "little grey cells," but he refused to grant the brain the right to be the sole determiner of what is true. A human being, Thomas recognized, is a hyphenation of cognition and emotion. So only when thinking and feeling are harnessed side by side, only when they are pulling together as a team, is a man or woman functioning as a complete person. We are a whole believer, then, when we are a doubting-believer.

DOUBTING-BELIEF—1954–1967—EGLWYS-FACH

On the way to my first meeting with Thomas, I decided to stop at Eglwys-fach, his parish from 1954 to 1967. A visit, I thought, could add to my understanding of the poems he wrote in the gaps between trying to please his Eglwys-fach parishioners, who were more demanding than his Manafon ones had been.

By the time I reached Eglwys-fach on an August Sunday in 1992 and found a place to park at St. Michael's Church, I was in no mood for absorbing poetic insights. During my drive, I had slowpoked along rain-lashed roads behind holidayers towing their own sleeping accommodations. Drizzle replaced the rain as I approached Eglwys-fach, but just as the day seemed to

3. Thomas, *Collected Poems 1945–1990*, 345; "Adjustments" ("Never known as anything").

be brightening, a car dragging an oversized camper forced me to brush my side mirror against a stone wall. The sound of splintering glass darkened my gray mood. Then, to my surprise, the color of the church's interior matched my own—black.

I didn't know it at the time, but St. Michael's black pulpit and black pews were my introduction to Elsi and Ronald Thomas. Elsi could not abide sheen of any kind, not even the glimmer of a bald man's head. So when she arrived at Eglwys-fach and found glossy varnish on the church's furnishings, she insisted it must go. Yielding, perhaps with a new vicar's misgivings about making hasty changes, Ronald sanded off the luster and painted the pews and pulpit matt-black.

Matt-black is emblematic of Thomas's years at Eglwys-fach, not because his ministry there was all darkness, though some of his days were blackened by his parishioners' attitudes and antics; but because matt-black gives visible expression to the concept of *nothing*, which, he says, became his obsession at Eglwys-fach. Black symbolizes the belief that there is *nothing* beyond the farthest reach of science. Black is the color of the belief that there is *no* God. Black also symbolizes experiences of the *absence* of God.

At Eglwys-fach, Thomas began to write poems that hold those *black* concepts in tension with concepts that may be visualized as *light*. In tension with the belief that there is *nothing* transcending the material universe, Thomas believed there is *Someone*. In opposition to those who said God *is not*, Thomas said God *is*. Finally, he united darkening experiences of God's *absence* with illuminating experiences of God's *presence*. Out of the tension between these dark and light concepts came Thomas's poetry of doubting-belief; poems that started to characterize the books he published during the period of his life that began with his move to Eglwys-fach.

If Thomas's time at Eglwys-fach disclosed another tension in his life, the hyphenation of doubt and belief, some of his old hyphenations faded, while others remained. Eglwys-fach, which was close to the river Dyfi and not far upstream from the ocean, was almost ideally located for a land-sea-sky man.

Sometimes Thomas could hear the water's roar, and "once every day the tide would come up the river and the tang of the sea could be smelt in the foam."[4] His new vicarage was "ugly," but the "district" he told a friend, "is superb."[5] "The hill-country rose immediately behind the main road, and foaming streams ran down the narrow valleys towards the few plains between sea and mountain."[6] For the first time since 1935, when he left Bangor, Thomas was in a place that contained what he loved best in nature. All that was missing was a sea view from his window.

While Thomas's move to Eglwys-fach largely satisfied his land-sea-sky identity, it did not ease the tension between his Cymric and Anglo identities. Yes, there were Welsh-speakers at Eglwys-fach. *But.* With every positive comment, Thomas grumbled a *but.* "The Welsh tends to be weak" at Eglwys-fach, Thomas told a friend, "but at least one speaks it every day, unlike Manafon where I never used it."[7] But the parish was dominated by English-speaking Welsh men and women and by English retirees who settled in Wales to stretch the buying power of their pounds. But Manafon's "smell of the farmyard was replaced by [Eglwys-fach's] smell of the decayed conscience."[8] But Thomas was pleased to have found a London publisher for his poems—poems in which he "said some sharp things about the English and the urban outlook."[9]

No matter where Thomas lived, he found Welsh people who weren't Welsh enough to pass his test of Welshness, and English people who had moved to Wales to take advantage of what Wales had to offer—lovely scenery, lower prices. And Thomas himself, self-appointed arbiter of Welshness, worried about the fluctuations of his world stock as an English-language poet.

---

4. Thomas, *Autobiographies*, 63.

5. Davies, *Thomas: Letters to Garlick*, 28.

6. Thomas, *Autobiographies*, 63.

7. Davies, *Thomas: Letters to Garlick*, 28.

8. Thomas, *Collected Later Poems 1988–2000*, 34; "There are sins rural and sins social."

9. Davies, *Thomas: Letters to Garlick*, 66.

Thomas's parish duties were heavier at Eglwys-fach than they had been at Manafon. His parishioners were better educated, rather sophisticated, and the boys from a nearby boarding school attended the Sunday morning service. Preparing sermons that would hold the attention of adolescents and simultaneously address adult concerns took more time than he was accustomed to devoting to that responsibility.

The fact that Thomas was a pacifist did not endear him to the retired military officers in his congregation, and his inability to suffer fools gladly caused him to lose hours of poetry-writing time dealing with blowbacks from his impolitic words and actions: "I spend most of my time coping with situations and trying to re-acclimatize myself to poetry in the brief intervals between."[10]

Just when Thomas's number of hours for writing poems was waning, the demand for new books of poetry from his pen was waxing. Several awards, including the Queen's Gold Medal for Poetry in 1964, gained him a growing number of readers. These were accompanied by critical voices mounting in volume, which caused him to fret about the quality of his work: "One gets pleased at the time [with a new poem] and then turns a sour look on the thing later," he told a friend.[11] And always there were the nibbles of the critical maggots: "I can imagine," he wrote the same friend, "what the critics will say if I publish another book." Then he quoted e. e. cummings' jibe about critics feasting upon poets, and declared: "It has a nice maggoty tang about it."[12]

LOCATED AT LAST—1967–1994—ABERDARON, RHIW

In 1967, Thomas and Elsi moved to Aberdaron, where he began to write his mature poems of doubting-belief. Perhaps this occurred because he had more time for writing. More likely, it was due to Aberdaron's tip-of-peninsula location—a place where infinite sky

10. Ibid., 45.
11. Ibid., 31.
12. Ibid., 56.

and infinite sea make it easier to believe that what grounds us is not geology but God.

Called "the remotest village in all Wales," Aberdaron clings to the end of the Llŷn peninsula, which Thomas called "a bough / of country that is suspended / between sky and sea."[13] In calm weather, small boats sail from its harbor to the island of Bardsey, which in the Middle Ages was a destination for men and women vowed to visit the graves of the island's saints.

Thomas's church stood at the bottom of Aberdaron, where the sea breaks wave upon wave against the rocky shore. Uphill from the church, the vicarage was exposed to the wind's capricious moods, but it afforded Thomas panoramic views of the tirelessly waving sea by day; and at night, when he was wakeful, there were "the sleepless conurbations / of the stars."[14] Welsh was the language of daily life, and many species of migratory birds made Aberdaron, to Thomas's delight, one of their ports of call.

When Thomas settled in Aberdaron, he hoped to speak Welsh daily and to emphasize his Welsh identity. As it turned out, Welsh was Aberdaron's everyday tongue. He was able to report that "both Church-wardens actually write to me in Welsh,"[15] and Welsh was "the main medium of daily life."[16] *But.* But Aberdaron's Welsh-speakers depended upon English tourists for their income. But Thomas himself was "in a bit of a jam . . . in having to write in English."[17]

Aberdaron came to know Thomas as a "Welsh Nationalist."[18] He campaigned for the use of Welsh in the registering of births and marriages, wanted the county council to send out official notices in Welsh, and argued for using Welsh on road signs and in shop

---

13. Thomas, *Collected Poems* 1945–1990, 503; "Retirement" ("I have crawled out at last").

14. Ibid., 296; "Alive" ("It is alive. It is you").

15. Davies, *Thomas: Letters to Garlick.*, 68.

16. Ibid., 69.

17. Ibid., 71.

18. Ibid., 77.

windows. *But.* "This part of Wales is a dead loss to nationalism, and yet they speak Welsh as their first language."[19]

Writing about his peninsular location, Thomas says, "Here was the marriage / of land and sea, from whose bickering / the spray rises."[20] There were a number of bickering marriages within Thomas's life, from which the spray of his poetry rose. One was the marriage of his Welsh and English identities; another, the marriage of his vocations as priest and poet.

As a priest, Thomas had an inner *bishop*; as a poet, an inner *muse*. The bickering between his bishop and his muse increased after he moved to Aberdaron, a village, as we have seen, at the head of a peninsula, where contemporary waves bicker with ancient rocks.

For Thomas, a priest in the Anglican tradition, the bishop represented ancient rock-like belief in God. The bishop guarded centuries-old orthodox doctrine and theology, received and handed on the traditions of Christian life and faith. The bishop, viewed as standing in a line extending back to the apostles, ordained persons to the priesthood, thereby conferring authority to break the eucharistic bread. Thomas's muse, on the other hand, represented contemporary responses to all that is. She was not tied to past ways of believing and thinking. Her voice doubted every theology that flouts today's best scientific and historical research. She ordained persons to the bardship, thereby conferring authority to break the bread of metaphoric truth.

After eleven years as vicar of the church of Saint Hywyn, Aberdaron, Thomas retired on the day after Easter of 1978. He and Elsi moved a few miles along the Llŷn peninsula's coast to Rhiw, where they settled into a three-centuries-old stone cottage that snuggles into the hillside across a narrow road from a bay called Hell's Mouth.

Thomas continued his avid support of the Welsh Nationalist cause, became a campaigner for the anti-nuclear movement, and

19. Ibid., 82.

20. Thomas, *Collected Later Poems 1988–2000*, 196; "Pen Llŷn" ("Dafydd looked out").

chaired a trust that purchased the island of Bardsey for the purpose of preserving its natural beauty and its Welsh and Christian heritages. And, of course, he continued to write poems and, after "consigning to the waste basket what I am not satisfied that the public should see,"[21] to publish them. One of these, "The Other," expresses Thomas's belief in the wakeful God.

Thomas, the priest, recalls the ancient Hebrew theme of the insomniac God—the Lord who "keeps Israel will neither slumber nor sleep"[22]—and ponders it anew in a peninsular location, where he lived in the presence of one metaphor for the *finite*, granite-based land, and two metaphors for the *infinite*, sky and sea.

> There are nights that are so still
> that I can hear the small owl calling
> far off and a fox barking
> miles away. It is then that I lie
> in the lean hours awake listening
> to the swell born somewhere in the Atlantic
> rising and falling, rising and falling
> wave on wave on the long shore
> by the village, that is without light
> and companionless. And the thought comes
> of that other being who is awake, too,
> letting our prayers break on him,
> not like this for a few hours,
> but for days, years, for eternity.[23]

While Thomas continued to be active, writing and publishing poems and taking stands on contemporary issues, Elsi, whose health had begun to fail while they lived at Eglwys-fach, became progressively weaker. In 1984, she "fell in the road and broke her thigh bone."[24] The loss of sight in one eye "makes her balance unstable."[25] In 1989, Thomas told a friend: "Elsi is in pretty poor

21. Davies, *Thomas: Letters to Garlick*, 120.

22. Ps 121:4.

23. Thomas, *Collected Poems 1945–1990*, 457; "The Other" ("There are nights that are so still").

24. Davies, *Thomas: Letters to Garlick*, 123.

25. Ibid., 123.

shape really and not improving, I'm afraid."[26] In March of 1992, in a letter Thomas wrote to help me plan my first trip to see him, he said: "I hope I remembered to say that the reason I can't offer much in the way of hospitality is that my wife died a year ago this month."

"I Know When, / But Where?"

There was no doubt in Thomas's mind about the date of Elsi's death, about when she died. But there was doubt about her destination, about where she was. In a memorial poem, he describes a fly failing to "Hold hard" to a rock:

> Here, gone, the raised wings
> a rainbow. She, too:
> here, gone. I know when,
> but where?[27]

The death of a loved one is a crack through which doubt often slips into one's life. Perhaps Elsi, whose life as a painter had a rainbow quality, is nowhere? Perhaps she has ceased to be?

Thomas tells us that he himself "woke up . . . to a consciousness / of when he was not, to / the equal certainty / of his being extinguished."[28]

Thomas, then, was not immune to the feeling that death is the end. But it was not his final position, which was his belief in God. And he believed, he told me, that God would decide what to make of Thomas after he died. That was all? That, he said, was enough.

And Elsi continued to come to him:

> . . . Impalpable,
> invisible, she comes
> to me still, as she would
> do, and I at my reading.

26. Ibid., 137.

27. Thomas, *Collected Later Poems 1988–2000*, 313; "In Memoriam: M.E.E." ("The rock says: 'Hold hard.'").

28. Ibid., 35; "An obsession with nothing."

There is a tremor
of light, as of a bird crossing
the sun's path, and I look
up in recognition
of a presence in absence.[29]

For Thomas, belief was the noun, doubt the modifier. Never did he cease believing in God. Never, too, did he become doubt free.

Not only couldn't Thomas become doubt free, he didn't want to be doubt free. For he recognized the positive role played by doubt. Doubt purifies belief by helping the believer cast off flawed ways of understanding and representing God. It strengthens belief by helping the believer think through and answer questions that the *seen* world raises about the *unseen* world. It takes questioning into belief, thereby enabling belief to resist unbelief more effectively.

Four Sources of Doubt

For the believer, there are four sources of doubt. The first is personal experiences such as the death of a loved one, divorce, job loss, failure to live up to one's goals, psychological depression—a host of dark nights of the spirit.

The second is science. Scientists simply do not need God as a working hypothesis. They direct their probing intellects through one evolutionary development after another until they come to the genesis moment of the universe, which, at this point in time, is called the Big Bang. Behind it—anything? No. That there is a universe is purely a matter of happenstance.

Scientists simply do not need God. Their calculations can proceed without the postulate of a supreme being, a Prime Mover, an Intelligent Designer. They are satisfied with *chance* as the answer to the question of why there is a universe and at least one planet populated with living things. They see no reason to tussle with Thomas's bedtime quandary:

29. Ibid., 237; "No Time" ("She left me. What voice").

> Promising myself before bedtime
> to contend more urgently
> with the problem. From nothing
> nothing comes. Behind everything—
> something, somebody?[30]

Thomas balked at the premise that *something* can come from *nothing*. Many scientists, on the other hand, balk at the believer's insistence that "Behind everything" there is "something, somebody." And this resistance on the part of many scientists to belief in God causes believers who take science seriously to question, even to doubt, their own belief.

History is the third source of doubt for believers. It narrates events that cause us to cry out, "Where was God while that was happening?" Three years after Thomas's birth, on the first day of the Battle of the Somme, approximately 58,000 British soldiers were killed. While he was in his late twenties and early thirties, roughly six million Jewish men, women, and children fell prey to Hitler's "final solution." When Thomas was 81, an estimated 800,000 persons were massacred in Rwanda.

"Where was God when all those atrocities were being committed?" Some reply, "Sleeping." Others declare, "There is no God."

Thomas looked at the Holocaust and the other unforgivable barbarities of his era and agreed that they stirred up doubts about God, but he never allowed his doubts to cancel his belief in the never slumbering God. Rather, Thomas used those doubts to refine his understanding of God as a God who created human beings with the freedom to love one another or to massacre one another; with the freedom to praise God, curse God, or thumb their noses at even the idea of God.

The fourth source of the believer's doubt is the Bible's God.

THE BIBLE'S GOD

The Bible's God is elusively present in human lives—a point made by the biblical authors, not with straightforward theological

30. Ibid., 263; "The Promise" ("Promising myself before bedtime").

statements, but by telling stories about men and women who experience God as unseeable, unpredictable, and unknowable— a self-concealing God.

The people of the Bible encounter God as an *unseeable* presence. When God is with Moses, all that Moses sees is a blazing shrub, from which comes a voice giving him a commission that can only come from God.[31] While the boy Samuel is lying down in the temple, he hears a voice calling his name, but the only speaker he can see, the priest Eli, has not spoken.[32] When Jesus, after he has been baptized by John, is coming up out of the Jordan, all he sees is a dove, but he hears these words: "You are my Son, the Beloved; with you I am well pleased."[33] In the Bible, when God is present, the deity is heard but not seen.

In addition to being unseeable, the God of the Bible is *unpredictable*. Biblical people are always being surprised by God. Suddenly, unannounced, God speaks to Moses, who is tending his father-in-law's sheep, and says, "I will send you to Pharaoh to bring my people, the Israelites, out of Egypt."[34] Suddenly, unheralded, God speaks to Amos, who is dressing sycamore trees at Tekoa, and says, "Go, prophesy to my people Israel."[35] Suddenly, unpredictably, as two women named Mary are standing at the tomb of Jesus, there is an earthquake and an angel rolls back the stone and says, "Do not be afraid."[36] Moments later, suddenly, as the two women are hurrying away, Jesus meets them and says, "Greetings!"[37] One thing is predictable about God: God is unpredictable.

Not only is *I Am* unseeable and unpredictable, the God of the Bible is also *unknowable*. At the burning bush, Moses asks for the name of the voice that is addressing him. The voice answers, "My

31. Exod 3:1–15.
32. 1 Sam 3:1–9.
33. Mark 1:9–11.
34. Exod 3:10.
35. Amos 7:14–15.
36. Matt 28:1–5.
37. Matt 28:9.

name is Yahweh,"[38] which means, among other possible translations, "I Shall Be Whoever I Shall Be." Then the Voice goes on to
say that "Yahweh," the One who is known as unknown, will be
his name "forever."[39] God is known as the One who everlastingly
eludes our attempts to know God. "I shall always be known to you,"
God tells us, "as the One who is unknowable to you." The essence
of Yahweh, precisely because it is divine, forever eludes our human
grasp. *I Am* colonizes the gaps in our knowledge.

Even when God is with us in the Man of Nazareth; even when
the Word of God has become flesh in Jesus the Christ, God remains unknowable. What we know of God in the life and words
of Jesus is elusive, because there are so many Jesuses. There is a
somewhat different Jesus in each of the four Gospels. And there
is the Jesus of liberal Protestants and the Jesus of fundamentalists;
the Jesus of Roman Catholics and the Jesus of Unitarians; the Jesus
of Greek Orthodoxy and the Jesus of Pentecostalism. Who Jesus is,
like who God is, remains a mystery, ultimately unknowable.

The unknowable, unpredictable, and unseeable God is
sometimes addressed as the hidden God. The psalmist complains:
"Why, O Lord, do you stand far off? Why do you hide yourself in
times of trouble?"[40] "Truly," Isaiah tells God, "you are a God who
hides himself."[41] Nailed to the cross, Jesus cries, "My God, my God,
why have you forsaken me?"[42]

Those words of Jesus echo in Thomas's poetry. "Why no!" he
exclaims,

> . . . I never thought other than
> That God is that great absence
> In our lives, the empty silence
> Within, the place where we go
> Seeking, not in hope to
> Arrive or find. He keeps the interstices

38. Exod 3:14.
39. Exod 3:15b.
40. Ps 10:1.
41. Isa 45:15.
42. Matt 27:46, Mark 15:34.

In our knowledge, the darkness
Between stars. . . .[43]

Often, for Thomas, God is hidden, but hidden, paradoxically, in a way that Thomas experiences as a presence. "It is this great absence," he writes,

> that is like a presence, that compels
> me to address it without hope
> of a reply. It is a room I enter
>
> from which someone has just
> gone, the vestibule for the arrival
> of one who has not yet come. . . .[44]

As in the Bible, so in Thomas's poetry: God is unseeable. But the unseeable God is experienced so powerfully, so intensely, that we are motivated to acknowledge that a spiritual void is all we have to offer to God. "What resource have I," Thomas asks, "other than the emptiness without him of my whole / being, a vacuum he may not abhor?"[45] When there is a hungering and thirsting emptiness at the core of our being, then the elusive God may, suddenly, become a God who fills us, perhaps even to overflowing.

Thomas presents this *suddenly*-present God in two poems titled "Suddenly." In the first of these, the title needs to be read as the first word of the poem:

> *Suddenly*
>
> As I had always known
> [God] would come, unannounced,
> remarkable merely for the absence
> of clamour. . . ."[46]

In the second of Thomas's "Suddenly" poems, God speaks with the tongues of nature:

43. Thomas, *Collected Poems* 1945–1990, 220; "Via Negativa" ("Why no! I never thought other than").
44. Ibid., 361; "The Absence" ("It is this great absence").
45. Ibid., 361; "The Absence" ("It is this great absence").
46. Ibid., 283, "Suddenly" ("As I had always known").

> Suddenly after long silence
> [God] has become voluble.
> He addresses me from a myriad
> directions with the fluency
> of water, the articulateness
> of green leaves. . . ."[47]

God is suddenly but also *fleetingly* present. "He is such a fast / God," Thomas observes, "always before us and / leaving as we arrive."[48] As in the Bible, so in Thomas's poems, God is unpredictable.

Finally, as in the Bible, so in the poetry of Thomas, God is unknowable. "The mind's tools," Thomas writes, have "no power convincingly to put [God] / together."[49] Therefore, Thomas suggests, there should be a "blank"—white space, *nothing*—beside the word "God" in our dictionaries.[50]

We have now seen that the God of the Bible is unseeable, unpredictable, and unknowable—hidden. The essence of God forever eludes the probes of our questioning intelligence. God refuses to be pinned down, declines to conform to the categories of the human mind.

Why?

WHY DOES GOD HIDE?

First, God hides to keep us from thinking we can prove the existence of God; hides to prevent us from supposing we can comprehend God. For a god whose existence is provable, whose existence is comprehensible, is a god we have configured and manufactured—an idol. The God who made us is a God who frustrates our most sophisticated efforts to prove that he is, to explicate what she is. As Thomas observes: We are "always on the verge of comprehending God, but insomuch as" we are mortal creatures, we "never will."[51]

47. Ibid., 426; "Suddenly" ("Suddenly after long silence").

48. Ibid., 364; "Pilgrimages" ("There is an island there is no going").

49. Ibid., 353; "Perhaps" ("His intellect was the clear mirror").

50. Ibid., 324; "The Gap" ("God woke, but the nightmare").

51 [51] Anstey, *R. S. Thomas: Selected Prose*, 131.

Thomas understood that our theological situation is one of "almosting it," to borrow words from Stephen Dedalus in James Joyce's *Ulysses*. Every doctrinal formula *almosts* God; every systematic theology *almosts* God. We live on the theological edge of understanding God, but because we are mortal, the best that we can do is *almost* it.

The second reason God hides is to draw us into a lifelong quest for God, because that which we cannot grasp has a way of grasping us. During the time when I was forming my R. S. Thomas collection, my must-find list included the first printings of his earliest books and a number of signed limited editions. Locating those items riveted my attention. "Will today's mail," I'd wonder, "bring a catalogue listing something I want?" Then, after finding a long-sought book, there was the excitement-filled waiting for the package to arrive, the careful removal of layer after layer of protective wrapping, and then, at long last, the book itself, which I catalogued and put on the shelf. At that point, the particular item lost its power to hold my attention. Because I had it, it no longer had me.

God, by refusing to be *had*, keeps us fascinated with God. God hides to shape us as lifelong pursuers of *more*: more understanding of what we can understand about God; more passion in our quest for a deeper relationship with God; more love of God, self, and others.

God's hiding, while preventing us from imagining that we understand God and while drawing us into a lifelong search for God, also makes us doubting-believers. For a God who is not pin-down-able is a God who is doubtable.

It is doubting-belief, then, that correlates with the God of the Bible—the hidden God. For a God who hides is a God who, by hiding, gives us freedom to doubt God. Indeed, a hidden God creates a situation in which it is in some sense natural to doubt God. So to be a doubting-believer is to believe in the God of the Bible—the unseeable God, the unpredictable God, the unknowable God; the God who is self-concealing.

R. S. Thomas: Doubting-Believer

Thomas believed in the God of the Bible—the God who, because he hides from our mind, elicits our doubt; the God who, because she touches our heart, elicits our belief. Responding to the biblical God, Thomas was a doubting-believer. Always, however, his belief was the noun, that which is substantive; his doubt was adjectival, the qualifier of belief.

We have looked at a number of Thomas's poems in which doubt comes to the fore. Here, in "Alive," belief dominates:

> It is alive. It is you,
> God. Looking out I can see
> no death. The earth moves, the
> sea moves, the wind goes
> on its exuberant
> journeys. Many creatures
> reflect you, the flowers
> your colour, the tides the precision
> of your calculations. There
> is nothing too ample
> for you to overflow, nothing
> so small that your workmanship
> is not revealed. I listen
> and it is you speaking.
> I find the place where you lay
> warm. At night, if I waken,
> there are the sleepless conurbations
> of the stars. The darkness
> is the deepening shadow
> of your presence; the silence a
> process in the metabolism
> of the being of love.[52]

Thomas is awestruck by his vision of the presence of God in creation. Indeed, awe is always the believer's proper response to God, Thomas insisted.

52. Thomas, *Collected Poems 1945–1990*, 296; "Alive" ("It is alive. It is you").

Not for him a palsy-walsy stroll with Jesus in a dew-bedecked garden. He thought that George Herbert, one of his favorite poets, was too buddy-buddy in his attitude toward God. But, we may ask, isn't familiarity with God, even love of God, biblical? "No," Thomas said, "loving God is too much of a human construct. What there must be is awe."[53]

Two centuries earlier, another Anglican priest, John Wesley, rejected the application of terms of endearment to God, and did not include his brother Charles's hymn "Jesus, Lover of My Soul" in his most comprehensive hymnbook. Referring to such words as "lover," John argued that their use displays an "odious and indecent familiarity" with God. It "damps," he said, the "speechless awe" that should characterize our relationship "with God our Creator, our Redeemer."[54]

The Palestinian Explosion with Endless Fallout

For Thomas, Jesus is God's "explosive" word to us:

> . . . What word so explosive
> as that one Palestinian
> word with the endlessness of its fall-out?[55]

Those three lines bring centuries of doctrinal statements about the Incarnation, about the Word of God becoming flesh,[56] into the world of atom bombs and nuclear power plants. They remind us that the sayings and actions of a man who lived in the outback of the Roman Empire two millennia ago continue to filter into the lives of men, women, and children.

Thomas provides the backstory to the Palestinian explosion in his poem "The Coming." He takes us into the transcendent realm, showing us what led "The son" to make a journey to planet

---

53. Rogers, *Man Who Went into the West*, 301.

54. *Works of John Wesley*, Vol. 4, 104.

55. Thomas, *Collected Poems 1945–1990*, 317; "Nuclear" ("It is not that he can't speak").

56. John 1:1, 14.

earth; what prompted the Word of God to become flesh in Jesus
of Nazareth:

> And God held in his hand
> A small globe. Look, he said.
> The son looked. Far off,
> As through water, he saw
> A scorched land of fierce
> Colour. The light burned
> There; crusted buildings
> Cast their shadows; a bright
> Serpent, a river
> Uncoiled itself, radiant
> With slime.
> On a bare
> Hill a bare tree saddened
> The sky. Many people
> Held out their thin arms
> To it, as though waiting
> For a vanished April
> To return to its crossed
> Boughs. The son watched
> Them. Let me go there, he said.[57]

---

57. Thomas, *Collected Poems* 1945–1990, 234; "The Coming" ("And God
held in his hand").

3

First Visit—1992

WE HAVE FOLLOWED R. S. Thomas from his birth to the year of my first visit. Along the way, we have looked at his hyphenated identities: Anglo-Cymric, a man of land-sea-sky, poet-priest, and doubting-believer. And we have gained the impression that often he was cantankerous, curmudgeonly, stony-faced. So what, I wondered, would I see when I sat across a dinner table from him. A face of stone or a face of flesh?

"AT THE SPEED OF CONCORDE"

Thomas did not answer my first letter, written in 1988, in which I described my collection of his works. Three years later, in May of 1991, shamelessly using my honorary doctorate, I enlisted the aid of an editor at Seren, a Welsh press that published several of Thomas's books: Was he willing, I asked, to let Thomas know that I planned to be in Oxford the following summer for a theological institute and would like to visit him? Within two months, Thomas responded:

> Y Rhiw, Pwllheli, Cymru (Wales)
> July 29, 1991
>
> Dear Dr McEllhenney
>
> Your letter to Seren Books eventually came my way. I did not hasten to answer it, as your visit seemed so far

off, but as time flies for an old man, I suppose it will be upon me at the speed of Concorde. I think the best thing would be for you to telephone me from Oxford to see how I am placed at that time.

Yn gywir iawn[1]
R. S. Thomas

Early in 1992, I asked Thomas these questions: Which of several dates do you prefer for my visit? What do you know about the Carreg Plas Guest House? Is it correct to assume that the poem titled "Gideon Pugh" is by you, not "S. R. Thomas," which is the way the journal *Wales* identifies the poet? And what is the denominational affiliation of the clergyman in your poem "The Minister"? Thomas answered:

Y Rhiw, Pwllheli, Cymru (Wales)
February 9, 1992

Dear Dr McEllhenney

Thank you for your letter. I leave the choice to you, as I am not committed at present. I have no knowledge of Carreg Plas as a guest house. All these places are run by English people, who no doubt [are] quite happy in the 'United Kingdom'.

I'm afraid I am more ignorant than you about denominations. I can't remember what The Minister's was supposed to be, nor can I remember Gideon Puw. My early work has had more than enough notice compared with the later. I hope you have read 'Counterpoint'.

Yours sincerely
R. S. Thomas

Thomas was not happy in the United Kingdom, which he saw as a union imposed upon Wales by its English conquerors. "Wales," he writes,

---

1. Thomas's complimentary closing may be translated as "Yours very truly," or "Sincerely yours," or something similar.

was conquered by the English and our best land taken away. . . . Our land today is being taken over by the English completely legally, according to English law, namely by means of money, and most of our fellow Welshmen do not care at all, so long as they make a profit.[2]

Thomas never used U.K. as part of the return address on his letters, preferring Cymru, the Welsh word for Wales. This signaled his view of Cymru as a distinct country, not a province of a larger one.

My next letter fixed August 11–12 as the time for my visit, and I asked Thomas to suggest a Welsh-owned inn instead of Carreg Plas. He responded almost immediately:

> Y Rhiw, Pwllheli, Cymru (Wales)
> March 8, 1992
>
> Dear Dr McEllhenney
>
> Thank you for your letter. No, we had better stick to your arrangement to stay at Carreg Plas. I meant it that all the hotels and guest houses are in English hands. This could have been a good thing, the serf mentality bred in the Welsh over centuries of English rule means that they prefer to skivvy for the English rather than risk running things themselves. I will make a note of August 11 and 12. This peninsula will be overrun with English visitors then, so you won't hear much Welsh. I hope I remembered to say that the reason I can't offer much in the way of hospitality is that my wife died a year ago this month.
>
> Yours sincerely,
> R. S. Thomas

Thomas's comment about Welsh people preferring "to skivvy for the English" reminds me of "Reservoirs," which we examined in chapter 1. Just as the Welsh allowed their "gravestones, chapels, villages even" to be swallowed up by the thirst of English cities for water, so have the Welsh subconsciously allowed their pride, their initiative, their willingness to take risks, to go down under the waves of English invaders.

2. Anstey, *R. S. Thomas: Selected Prose*, 116.

Three parts of my next letter need to be quoted in order to understand Thomas's reply:

> From the map sent by the innkeeper, Carreg Plas appears to be north of Aberdaron, about 2 miles, and close to the Whistling Sands.
>
> Could you give me the name and address of someone to contact to work out a way to see the interior of the Church of St. Michael and All Angels, Manafon, on Friday, 14 August?
>
> Recently, while confined to bed with a bout of labyrinthitis, I listened time and again to your 1976 recording. With the result that I thought a stop at Llanrhaeadr ym Mochnant might be interesting. And what about the churches you served at Chirk and Hanmer?

Thomas, for the first time, typed his answer, although both the salutation and the complimentary closing are handwritten:

> Y Rhiw, Pwllheli. Cymru (Wales)
> May 21, 1992
>
> Dear Prof. McEllhenney
>
> Thank you for your letter which I hasten to answer, as I shall be away until the beginning of June. I had not heard of labyrinthitis, which I should have thought was peculiar to the Minotaur. I will come to Carreg Plas on the Tuesday evening for dinner. Thank you. Porthor is the name of the beach. Whistling sands is English cheek; not even with their tongue in it.
>
> Your suggested itinerary seems rather circumambulatory to me; but then I have lost interest in the anglicised areas I once served in.
>
> If you wrote to Mrs. Ruth Hall, The Smithy, Manafon, POWYS, she would probably be able to arrange for the church to be open.
>
> Yours sincerely,
> R. S. Thomas

I wrote to Mrs. Hall, who told me to pick up the church key at her house when I reached Manafon. Meanwhile, I sent Thomas my final travel plans and noted that "labyrinthitis is peculiar to persons who are prone to sinus infections."

SOMEWHERE ALTOGETHER ELSEWHERE?

My next attempt to reach Thomas was by phone from Carreg Plas on August 11, the evening he promised to join me for dinner. I dialed his number. No answer. Waited. Tried again. Waited. Dialed once more. Had I traveled all this way to meet a man who, like his God, was somewhere altogether elsewhere? Then, minutes before seven o'clock, Thomas answered his phone, asked if I'd been trying to reach him, and explained that he had just returned from being hospitalized in Bangor. The National Health Service had been unable to give him a firm date for his elective hernia surgery, but the surgeon worked him in to get him home in time for my visit. He couldn't come to dinner, but would be at Carreg Plas the next morning at 11:30.

Arriving as promised, Thomas unfolded himself from his battered white VW hatchback, feathers of white hair flying, and asked me, because he was recovering from surgery, to use my car for our drive around the Llŷn peninsula. When I turned the ignition key, his voice boomed from the tape deck's speaker; I'd forgotten to switch it off the day before. Thomas was amused.

Apologizing for not being able to offer me home hospitality, he gave me lunch at the Woodlands Hall Hotel: poached salmon with prawns and Blue Nun Liebfraumilch. Although his demeanor was dry, he savored sweet wines. As I studied him, face to face, across the narrow table, his eyes seemed small, sharp, like those of the birds he watched. When he spoke, he pressed his palms into the deep depressions in his cheeks.

After lunch, he provided precise directions as I drove to Sarn-y-Rhiw, the stone, partially whitewashed cottage a few miles from Aberdaron, to which he and Elsi moved in 1978; it snuggles into a hillside across a narrow road from Porth Neigwl, "Hell's Mouth."

Elsi's health continued to decline after their move to Y Rhiw, but R. S. was, as we have seen, active in agitating for road signs in the Welsh language, joining the local branch of the Campaign for Nuclear Disarmament, chairing the Bardsey Island Trust Council, and helping found a community newspaper.

Elsi Thomas was hospitalized in early March 1991; when R. S. brought her home, he carried her up the stairs to her bedroom, where she died on March 10. Thomas showed me that room as we walked through his cottage. His own combination bed-sitting room is a modern addition to the three-centuries-old cottage, more spacious, sunnier and warmer than the rest of the tiny, stone-floored house. Shoes were stationed at his bed and chair, which was surrounded by books on the floor. There was no television set and only Welsh papers.

He noted that when he read, he simply absorbed some things without making any effort to stock his memory, which he called poor. Then, often after thirty minutes or so of reading, when he sensed the approach of his muse, he would put down the book, pick up pen and paper, lay down the first line of a new poem and wait to see how its sounds, and meter would shape the following lines.

Late afternoon, we drove into Aberdaron and walked through the Church of Saint Hywyn, which he served as vicar from 1967 to 1978. I asked him to allow me to photograph him standing in the pulpit. He replied, with his face of stone, that he never stepped into a pulpit without wearing his cassock and clerical collar.

He remarked that the Church in Wales had made his life possible, providing income in three country parishes, where he was free to read and write in the morning, walk the moors in the afternoon, and visit parishioners in the evening. They talked trivialities, which allowed him to learn to know them, so he could better minister to them in their times of need.

His parishioners, he said, were, by and large, "simple people," not readers of books. So he made his sermons simple, easy to understand. The byproduct of preaching to simple people, he suggested, is poetry that is not complex, not hard to grasp. Because

I am uninclined to challenge someone I've just met, especially someone whose writings have delighted and inspired me for two decades, I didn't contradict Thomas. But I see his poems as simple, yes, but simply brilliant in the way they unfold one implication after another as I ponder their words, follow their rhythms, listen to their sounds.

Thomas insisted that while the Church had given him a living, he had given the Church—the denomination as distinguished from his parishes—nothing in return. And the Church, perhaps responding in kind, paid little or no attention to him as a poet. The Archbishop of Wales once took the chair, he recalled, when he was reading his poems, and English Bishop George K. A. Bell mentioned him on some vaguely remembered occasion.

Late afternoon, we drove back to Carreg Plas for tea, more conversation, then a dinner of roast beef and Yorkshire pudding. Thomas left at 9:15—a long day for a seventy-nine-year-old, who used both of his somewhat shaky hands to lift a cup of coffee; who had been hospitalized until the day before. The nurses, he told me, his face of flesh grinning, were pretty Welsh girls, but when they spoke, they mixed in English words with their poor Welsh.

JOTTINGS

Thomas said many things during the nine hours we were together; not, however, in the form of an interview. So when he left, I quickly jotted down everything I could recall.

There had never been a time, he said, when he did not believe in God—not "a God," however, but "God." His theology of God, he added, was shaped by Søren Kierkegaard and Paul Tillich, his "favorite theologian." From Kierkegaard, he learned that God is not to be thought of as the object at the end of a line of reasoning; not "a being," albeit a supernatural one, among other beings, but rather Being itself. Thomas thought that Tillich's term for God, the "Ground of Being," was a good way to express his own thinking. God is the depth dimension, the transcendent dimension, of who we are and where we are.

Later, back home, I inserted in my notebook these sentences from one of Thomas's prose writings:

> With our greatest modern telescope we look out into the depths of space, but there is no heaven there. With our supersonic aircraft we annihilate time, but are no nearer eternity. May it not be that alongside us, made invisible by the thinnest of veils, is the heaven we seek?[3]

Heaven grounds us from within, not from above or below. God is here, "made invisible by the thinnest of veils."

Thomas acknowledged that his theology raises questions, one of which is: If God is the Ground of Being, then all beings—cyclones and cyclamens, saints and sadists, viruses and vitamins—have their grounding in God. This grounding permits Thomas to echo the prophet Joel, whose God directs the people of Israel to consider "the great army, which I sent against you"—the army of crop-eating insects: "the swarming locust, the hopper, the destroyer, the cutter."[4] Thomas's God asks haughty humans where their technological innovations will take them

> . . . from the invisible
> Viruses, the personnel
> Of the darkness that do my will?[5]

Thomas employed "secondary causation" to deal with the problem of "the invisible / Viruses" and the Ground of Being. He thought that God created a universe in which there are bacteria and auto accidents and homicidal maniacs. God does not micromanage this universe, deciding whom to invade with a pathogen, whom to spare; whom to pluck uninjured from a crash, whom to be pronounced dead at the scene. All those occurrences are matters of secondary causation—the eventual outcomes of the workings of nature's fundamental laws.

3. Ibid., 120.

4. Joel 2:25.

5. Thomas, *Collected Poems* 1945–1990, 230; "Soliloquy" ("And God thought: Pray away").

So it is pointless, Thomas thought, to pray for rain: God does not dispatch it in response to those who pray for it with the greatest zeal; it falls, or fails to fall, in accord with the atmospheric laws of an orderly creation. All of which means, he admitted, that intercessory prayer was a problem for him; as it is for all doubting-believers.

Believers crave certainty that God is concerned with their personal well-being. They desire assurance that God provides motherly comfort and love; that God supplies fatherly rescue from desperate situations. Doubters question why God, if God is good and loving, saves one good, believing person from cancer, while allowing another to suffer and die.

Thomas recognized that there is no way to answer both the questions of doubters and the cravings of believers. So he, as a doubting-believer, simply hyphenated his experiences of God's personal presence and his understanding of the operation of secondary causation in such matters as renal failure and rain. In his poem "Emerging," he says that "It begins to appear" that prayer is not about begging God for this or that. Rather, "It is the annihilation of difference, / the consciousness of myself in you [God], / of you in me."[6]

Continuing with my jottings: Thomas told me he hated organs, much preferring the unaccompanied human voice. In other references to music, he said he didn't like "the moderns"—not much, in fact, "after Mozart." Somewhat later, he added that he liked Schubert and Benjamin Britten, but not Britten's vocal music.

When celebrating the Eucharist, he refused to stand behind the table facing the congregation, because he understood the role of the priest to be that of an intermediary between the people and God. Therefore he took his place between the congregation and the table, leading the people up into the awe-inspiring presence of God. In his book titled, in English translation, *A Year in Llŷn*, Thomas is explicit:

---

6. Ibid., 263; "Emerging" ("Not as in the old days I pray").

> The new order of the Church in Wales has changed the whole atmosphere of Holy Communion for me. The pinnacle of the original service was when I, as a priest, would say the words of consecration over the bread and wine, with my back to the congregation as one who had the honour of leading them to the throne of God's grace.[7]

Thomas felt that standing behind the table, facing the people, tends to drain the sacrament of mystery: "It is to God that mystery belongs, and woe to man when he tries to interfere with that mystery."[8] It's a matter, as we saw in chapter 2, of awe. Familiarity with God "damps," in John Wesley's words, the "speechless awe" that should characterize our relationship "with God our Creator, our Redeemer." Thomas insists that "loving God is too much of a human construct. What there must be is awe."

Thomas mentioned that the University of Arkansas Press was bringing out a volume of essays about his work. Edited by William V. Davis and titled *Miraculous Simplicity: Essays on R. S. Thomas*, it was published in 1993. Also he noted that Wynn Thomas was editing a book about him. It marked his eightieth birthday, in 1993, and is titled *The Page's Drift: R. S. Thomas at Eighty*.

Picking up on the Arkansas Press volume, I asked: Have you visited the States? "No," spoken in a tone suggesting it was a place he did not care for. Perhaps the States epitomized all Thomas meant by the machine—a life in bondage to technology. Also the American craving for everything fast may have alienated Thomas, for he spoke wistfully of the time when men walked, and walking, garnered wisdom.

When walking people reached the sea, it seemed overwhelming, unknowable, mysterious—like God. When they began to fly over the ocean, it lost its mysterious powers. When walking people went on pilgrimage, it was the laborious walk itself that made them wiser, perhaps holier, before they reached the shrine. Now, flying people arrive too quickly to do anything other than listen to a guide's spiel and click pictures. We need to learn, Thomas

7. Thomas, *Autobiographies*, 131.
8. Ibid.

observes, "from the lichen's slowness / at work something of the slowness / of the illumination of the self."[9]

Those words highlight the fact that Thomas was more at home in the natural world than in the manufactured world. For him, the times in which we live are dominated by the Machine. In the Machine-world, transcendence gives way to technology; money buys and sells mystery. Thomas writes that he "was doubtful whether, in an industrial town, he could have worshipped and continued to believe. That is, the countryside was indispensable to his faith."[10]

Talking further about the United States, Thomas recalled an invitation to spend time at Amherst College and at a place in California run by a "nuclear physicist with an Italian name," but he had no desire to live in either place, away from his seaside cottage and his birdwatching. "It is too late," he once wrote, "to start / For destinations not of the heart."[11]

Continuing my questioning, I asked if he read novels. Yes; Henry James, Tolstoy, Dostoyevsky, Steinbeck. He said he loved Shakespeare, opting for reading his plays rather than seeing them staged. In a poem dealing with his taste in poetry, he wrote:

> But Shakespeare's cut and thrust,
> I allow you, was a must
>
> on my bookshelves; . . .[12]

Talking about poetry, he noted that he was an only child, a solitary one, who got up at dawn to wander in the fields; to which experiences he attributed his early delight in the poetry of Tennyson. In school, he went on, when he won a prize, he asked for a book of poems.

I asked him whose poetry he read now. Americans: Robert Frost, Wallace Stevens (his favorite), Robert Penn Warren, John

---

9. Thomas, *Collected Later Poems 1988–2000*, 63; "The pretenses are done with."

10. Thomas, *Autobiographies*, 84.

11. Thomas, *Collected Poems 1945–1990*, 120; "Here" ("I am a man now").

12. Ibid., 284, "Taste" ("I had preferred Chaucer").

Berryman. From Thomas's side of the Atlantic: Geoffrey Hill, Ted Hughes, Seamus Heaney.

"I prefer French poetry to Welsh," he noted, naming Charles Baudelaire. By coincidence, I was reading an article about Baudelaire when Thomas pulled up at Carreg Plas that morning. It quoted Baudelaire's "Dream of a Curious Man":

> I was a child, eager to see a play,
> Hating the curtain standing in the way . . .[13]

Like that child, I had been waiting for the curtain to go up on R. S. Thomas, restive at the fact that it had taken so long for me to see him face to face. Then the curtain lifted: He was with me. No longer was he somewhere, altogether elsewhere. Twice, I sat across a narrow table from Thomas, watching him press his palms into the deep depressions in his cheeks. His face of stone was being hyphenated for me with his face of flesh, which occasionally broke into a smile, even an impish one. I heard the vibrations of his vocal cords, not the sound of a tape machine reproducing his voice. I listened to his thoughts on a variety of topics. But as those things were happening, I began to realize that Thomas was there, and not there; an absence in a presence. The curtain had lifted, but, as in Baudelaire's poem, "I was waiting still."

Had I expected, I wondered, that I could look into the eyes of Thomas and see his muse? Whatever my anticipations, it became clear, during my nine hours with him, that there was more of Thomas in reserve than in revelation. I could grasp his hand, but he himself was ungraspable. The curtain had gone up, I had seen Thomas's face of flesh as well as his face of stone. Yet I had not seen the whole Thomas.

To a certain degree, Thomas was always somewhere altogether elsewhere.

---

13. Baudelaire, *The Flowers of Evil*, 281.

ANOTHER VISIT?

Following my visit with Thomas in August of 1992, I thanked him for his gift of himself on a day when he was recovering from surgery. In October, he sent me a signed copy of his new book of poems *Mass for Hard Times*. He had told me in August that he had suggested that the cover feature a tipped-over eucharistic chalice out of which pours a stream of English pound coins. After reading and rereading the book, I thanked him, singled out certain poems, and told him that my wife and I and several other couples would like to invite him to spend a day or two with us in Aberdyfi in May of 1993.

His reply, written on a plain card, seemed somewhat ambiguous, but for the first time he signed "R. S." instead of "R. S. Thomas."

4

Second Visit—1993

IN SOME CASES, R. S. Thomas's poems begin before the poem's opening line. To nudge us to read the title as the first word? To include us in an ongoing conversation? To hint that he wrote something before the first sentence of the completed poem, then struck it out, leaving it to us to listen for the ghost words?

Something like the latter is the case with the postcard he sent in response to my invitation to meet again, this time at Aberdovey, in May of 1993. These, perhaps, are Thomas's ghost words: *I have no commitments for early May. But I forgot to say* thank you for your card and enclosures.

> Y Rhiw. Pwllheli. Cymru.
> [no date, no postmark]
> [received February 8, 1993]
> [no salutation]
>
> Thank you for your card and enclosures. I shall no doubt hear details about your visit later on. Aberdyfi is not the best of centres from some points of view.
>
> Good wishes in '93
> R. S.

R. S. responded as a poet to one of my "enclosures," which was the letter of a historian. Poets favor the allusive; historians, the conclusive. I wanted a clear-cut answer to my question. R. S.

responded with an implied yes—Yes, I can meet you, and "shall no doubt hear details about your visit later on."

"We shall be traveling in a small bus with a driver," I told him. "On Wednesday, May 5, we anticipate a sightseeing drive in the Aberdovey area. It would be a rare privilege for us if you are willing to ride with us and help us see Wales through your eyes."

Thomas did not allow me to get away with the English spelling of Aberdovey. His correction, however, was gentle. He simply including the correct Welsh spelling in an observation about my sightseeing plan: "Aberdyfi is not the best of centres from some points of view."

He may have been nudging me to ask him for a better center, but too many pieces of the itinerary were in place to allow for an exchange of letters that could well end with Thomas saying, "No, we had better stick to your arrangements."

Aberdyfi must do.

I moved ahead with details, working on the assumption that Thomas had accepted my invitation. But when he did not answer my next two letters, and when the innkeeper in Aberdyfi pressed me to confirm that I needed a room for Thomas, I wrote again. No reply. Was Thomas imitating his often unresponsive God? Perhaps I should try the telephone? Thomas answered and said he planned to meet us at Aberdyfi.

And so he did, but . . .

WAITING

The sky was blue as ten of us traveled through Chesterfield, England, with its church spire pointing crookedly upward towards God. On the day we expected to meet Thomas, that spire was a Thomasian metaphor: All human reaching toward God is off plumb, askew.

Next, we visited Chatsworth, the country house of the dukes of Devonshire. Could Thomas have composed his poems in one of its large rooms? I doubt it. He chose remote parishes and small houses, because he recognized that constricted physical space is the right nursery for a developing spiritual vision.

After we crossed into Wales, the Welsh road signs confounded the English driver of our small bus. Which way, he wondered, is Aberdovey? Because Thomas had corrected my spelling, I pointed him in the direction of Aberdyfi.

Liz, the chef and one of the innkeepers at the Maybank Hotel in Aberdyfi, assured me that Thomas was in town. Because our five couples filled the Maybank's rooms, he was staying at another inn. He told her he would walk up the hill to join us for dinner.

The bath used by Patti and Dale was across the hall from their room, is always locked from the outside, and there's only one key. So when Dale returned to his room, forgetting to pick up the key from the edge of the washbowl, there was a minor crisis, to which Paul, the other innkeeper, responded with muttered frustration and a screwdriver.

Another Thomasian metaphor: The key to God is locked up inside God—"Truly, you are a God who hides himself."[1]

We gathered in the bar at 7:45 to greet Thomas. Minutes ticked by. No Thomas. We talked as you talk when worrying that the person you are expecting is somewhere altogether elsewhere. More minutes leaked away. Then, about 8:15, Thomas walked in, saying that he'd been waiting for a call from our English innkeeper. She, however, said she called him after we arrived to tell him when to join us.

Ducking the crossfire between a prickly Welsh nationalist and a proud English innkeeper, I quickly introduced Thomas to Louise and Charlie, Patti and Dale, Mannie and Bob, and Jean and Chuck. When I came to my wife, Nancy, he recalled that her mother had died while I was in England and Wales the previous year. The poet-priest so often portrayed as stone-faced, dour, was a thoughtful, caring man.

Menus were handed out. Thomas asked, with more than a hint of scepticism, "Is it Welsh lamb?" Promised that it was, he placed his order. He was "a very good eater," someone later recalled,

1. Isa 45:15

48

"never left a scrap of meat." During the meal, he spoke about the "Red Indians," his way of designating Native Americans. He saw parallels between the dispossession of the Native Americans by the European invaders and the dispossession of the Welsh by the English invaders.

Continuing to talk about America, Thomas called Wallace Stevens "the finest American poet," just as Henry James is "the finest novelist"; and he indicated he liked Edgar Lee Master's *Spoon River Anthology.*

The next morning, when the Dyfi estuary was mirroring an azure sky, Patti gave Thomas credit for the sparkling weather. "But," he replied, "I ordered mermaids." Some minutes later, as we studied the breakfast menu, Bob asked Thomas about black pudding. "It may make you dizzy," he answered. Bob wanted to know more, so Thomas suggested, "We'll both order it and see who keels over first." In short order, Thomas was breakfasting on sausage, bacon, and black pudding, with toast and tea. Bob said little about the black, pig's blood, pudding. Somehow the subject of hoagies, or sub sandwiches, came up, and Thomas wondered what they were. After we described slices of ham, salami, capicola, pepperoni, and provolone, plus lettuce, tomatoes, onions, and peppers, all stuffed into a long hard roll, he said, "How do you get into them? With a buzz saw?"

The Poet as Tour Guide

Mid morning, we boarded our bus, and Thomas sat beside the driver to navigate. We drove along the shores of Cardigan Bay, then turned inland, with Cader Idris, the storied Welsh mountain, straight ahead.

Thomas pointed our driver onto a single-track road that petered out at the little Welsh church of Llanfihangel-y-Pennant. It was from here, Thomas told us, that, in 1804, a girl named Mary Jones began a long walk across the mountains to Bala to obtain a Bible, a quest that inspired the formation of the British and Foreign Bible Society.

Our next Welsh history stop was at the ruins of Castell-y-Bere, an ancient Welsh fortress that was taken by the English in 1283, rebuilt by Edward I, and retaken by Welsh insurgents in 1295. Doubtless it was the latter event that appealed to Thomas— a castle built by an English king that was captured by Welsh partisans. As we walked up to the remains of the castle, I noticed some lambs and quoted to Thomas the rhyme in his poem "The Priest": "lambs cushion / His vision."[2] He responded by saying that the English language is particularly versatile for the writing of poems.

Time and again on our castle walk, he lifted his powerful field glasses to get a good look at a bird whose music he recognized, who had just returned as a herald of springtime.

We drove along a lake, Tal-y-Llyn, and on to the town of Dolgellau, where Thomas told our driver to turn onto a single-track road. As we Americans were enjoying the views, Thomas realized that he had picked the wrong turning. Back to Dolgellau, where he asked for directions, which brought us to another single-track road, on which we stopped again and again for Bob to get out, open a gate, wait for us to drive through, then close it, and get back on the bus. Soon the road plunged steeply downward, and the odor of hot brakes seeped into the bus. Our destination, perhaps chosen by Thomas to rib his American tourists, was the George III pub at a toll bridge over the river Mawddach. Thomas treated me to a pint of bitter; each of us had steak and kidney pie, chips, and peas.

To be with Thomas was to be enmeshed in paradox: lunch with a Welshman who spoke highly refined English, at a pub named for an English monarch, on a river with a Welsh name, eating quintessential English pub grub.

After lunch, we drove to the Craft Center at Corris, where Thomas looked for a jeweler who worked with Welsh gold. Did he, I wondered, have someone special in mind? On to Machynlleth and a stop at the house in which Owain Glendwr, during an

2. Thomas, *Collected Poems 1945–1990*, 196; "The Priest" ("The priest picks his way").

early-fifteenth-century attempt to regain independence for Wales, is said to have convened a Welsh parliament.

An hour or so after getting back to the Maybank, when Thomas had not appeared at the planned time, I walked down to his hotel. He said he had napped, indeed over-napped.

When we joined the others gathered in the Maybank lounge, Thomas sat deep in an uneasy-looking easy chair, and, using my copy of a book of his poems, read for us: "Pisces," "The Return," "In a Country Church," "Evans," "Meet the Family," "Souillac: Le Sacrifice D'Abraham," "The Moor," "In Church," and a number of other poems. Someone recalled later that "his personal reading of his poems sounded exactly like the tape we listened to on the bus—deep tones." Afterwards, he signed copies of his *Collected Poems 1945–1990*, which had just been published, commenting that he much prefers reading his poems to intimate groups such as ours.

Thomas repeated his meat choice of the previous night—Welsh lamb. At the close of the meal, the waiter carried in a cake with candles to observe Thomas's eightieth birthday, which was March 29, and my fifty-ninth, which was the day before.

Thomas talked about poetry at breakfast the next morning, observing that "a poet can be faulted for publishing too many poems, but not for writing too many." Taking on his critics, he suggested that they were faddish in their criticisms. "They complain about me never having written a *long* poem, seeming to think you cannot be truly great unless you, like some of today's popular poets, have written a sustained tour-de-force." He continued: "Before the publication of *H'm* [1972], they complained of my obsession with hill farmers. Since then, they have complained about my lack of form. They do not like sentences that run on from line to line." His rebuttal was that "form or shape is simply on the page for the eye." Then he talked about how poems come to him: "They take form in my mind. By the time I put them down on paper, they have almost final shape. I may on occasion change a word or two."

After breakfast, Thomas shook hands with each of us as we boarded our bus. When we were ready to leave, he ran up to the top of the hill where he could see oncoming traffic. When all was

clear, he beckoned our driver to pull out and away, then came lop-
ing back down the hill, waving goodbye.

OUR TOUR GUIDE REMEMBERED

Two days after leaving Aberdyfi, the ten of us Americans sat down
in the lounge of an English hotel to record our memories of two
days with a Welsh poet, who often is seen as stony-faced and
reclusive. "R. S.'s territory is beautiful," one said, "different, fantas-
tic." "He speaks few words, but they are well chosen." "His hands
are large." "He often walked the sand dunes when he was vicar of
Eglwysfach." "He has a sourpuss demeanor, yet is a warm, generous
person." "He was aware of each of us, did not lose the individual
in the crowd, said a personal goodbye to everyone." "He was very
much aware of everything: the music of birds, the least and the last,
the Welsh and the English." "He has a great sense of humor, can rib
and take a ribbing. Often there is a twinkle in his eye, a smile on his
face, a chuckle in his voice." "He seemed to enjoy his time with us."

I remembered that when I alluded to his image of "the sun
that cracks the cheeks / Of the gaunt sky perhaps once in a week,"[3]
he said he was referring to the Borders, the region along the Welsh-
English frontier, where he served his two curacies. Certainly, it was
true of Thomas himself: A smile cracked his gaunt cheeks rarely,
but radiantly.

Louise talked with Thomas about birds, remembering in particular their conversation about grey herons. She also said she got
the feeling from Thomas that he says to himself, "I'm eighty and so
can think and speak as I please." Someone else got the impression
that he is "open, very liberal, and does not like narrow-minded
people." Yet, another interjected, "he is narrow on Wales, on the
English." "He's a typical Welshman—doesn't like the English,
cynical about them, resents their interference." Also he is both
liberal and narrow on church-related matters. "He does not believe the only way to God is through Jesus." But when it comes to

---

3. Ibid., 4; "A Peasant" ("Iago Prytherch his name, though, be it allowed").

translations of the Bible, he much prefers the King James Version to modern ones, criticizing modern translators for lacking rhythm in their phrasing and a poet's ear in their word choices.

Because the five American men were clergy, we asked Thomas questions about his ministry as a priest of the Church in Wales. He commented that "the Church in Wales is run by a committee, and most of what it does is fiddle-faddle." To it, he said, he "owes nothing."

Although he speaks Welsh, it is not his first language. And since poetry, he thought, can only be written in one's first language, and since the language of the Bible and the Book of Common Prayer is poetic in nature, he has the right to critique English versions of those books, but not Welsh ones.

With regard to his own ministry, he remarked that except for Lent, he only had Sunday services, and he visited his parishioners when "he felt like it." He said he never went "into the pulpit to speak to the five or six in his congregation" He simply stood in the aisle, took a text, and talked about it for five or ten minutes." During his twelve years at Manafon, he "had three weddings and a few baptisms"—he did not recall how many.

Jean suggested to him that Nancy and I could find him a nook in the United States where he could be creative. "I'll probably get mugged, too," he replied.

At some point, I said to him, "I have always associated your poem 'The Prisoner' with Dietrich Bonhoeffer." "Pass, McEllhenney." "With what degree?" Chuck asked. "Poor second." "Never," Chuck rebutted. It is a joy to have loyal friends such as Chuck, but Thomas was correct. Only bare-bones knowledge of twentieth-century religious history was required to associate Thomas's poem with Bonhoeffer, Hitler's prisoner, who was hanged during the last days of the Third Reich.

A Masterwork of Doubting-Belief

BACK TO WRITING LETTERS

Three days after flying back to Philadelphia, I wrote to Thomas:

> West Chester, PA
> May 12, 1993
>
> Dear R. S.
> . . . .
> At the close of our time in England and Wales, when we reviewed our memories, we agreed that the time with you at Aberdyfi was the high point. Thank you for your willingness to be with us, talk with us, travel with us in Cymru, and read a number of your poems for us.
>
> In a separate package, I am sending you the third volume of Tillich's systematics. I remember hearing him lecture at my seminary, dealing, as I recall, not with systematic theology, but with his interest in poetry and the graphic arts. He said that Grünewald's painting of the resurrection is the only one that comes close to giving the right material form to that spiritual reality.
> . . . .
> Sincerely,
> John

Thomas did not deal with my comments about Tillich and Grünewald's "Resurrection" in his reply, but he did acknowledge the Tillich volume and alluded to my plan to write a book for pastors about his poetry:

> Y Rhiw. Pwllheli. Cymru. (Wales)
> [no date]
> postmarked June 5, 1993
>
> Dear John
>
> I keep on meaning to send you 'FRIEZE' – the book of poems I mentioned, but the arrival of Tillich's third volume this morning suggested that I had better send this before any more procrastination. I got your kind letter and hope that your projected book is eventually

54

published. I enjoyed showing your colleagues around my country, and I had a kind letter of appreciation from Bob. I have been busy lately giving readings here and there and conducting interviews.

With again thanks for the book from your own library

R. S.

A month later, I told Thomas about a book-purchasing misadventure:

Perhaps you will smile a sardonic smile at this mono-glot's dilemma. In Brecon, I saw a copy of *A History of Wales* by John Davies. Because it was thick and heavy, I decided not to carry it back to the States. But returning, I placed an order, only to [receive] a copy of *Hanes Cymru* by John Davies. Now, Chuck Yrigoyen, whom you met at Aberdyfi, will carry it to Cambridge later this month and attempt to exchange it for the English translation.

With that letter I enclosed an article, published in *Methodist History*, that was a reworking of a paper I read at the Oxford Institute of Methodist Theological Studies just before visiting Thomas at Aberdaron the previous summer. Thomas used a plain white card to respond:

Y Rhiw. Pwllheli. Cymru (Wales)
[no date, no postmark]
[no salutation]

Many thanks for your letter and enclosure. Sorry you had Welsh inflicted on you at much cost. I have nearly finished Tillich. I savour such wine slowly.

Regards
R. S.

My next letter deals with a number of topics, among which is Thomas's indignation when a man who could not speak Welsh was appointed to his former parish at Aberdaron:

A Masterwork of Doubting-Belief

West Chester, PA
September 20, 1993

Dear R. S.

Thank you for your post card. I'm pleased that you have been savouring the Tillich volume.

A friend, the chaplain of Robinson College, Cambridge, sent me a clipping from the *Sunday Telegraph* of September 5, in which the appointment of the Rev. Christopher Armstrong to Aberdaron is described and your reaction reported.

Before long, I expect to send to a publisher my detailed outline of the book I would like to write about the value of your poetry for pastors. . . .

Nancy and I are eagerly anticipating our son's marriage on October 16. Peter and Suzanne met at Oberlin College six years ago. We liked her very much the first time we spent a few hours together. . . .

I am enclosing the catalogue of my R. S. Thomas Collection; you asked me at Aberdyfi about several items. You can see the big holes – . . . .

Thomas replied immediately:

Y Rhiw
September 29, 1993

Dear John
Such industry! Phew. Puts me to shame. Like the Chinaman who clapped after the orchestra had finished tuning up, I applaud before the thesis gets written.

Yours sincerely
R. S.

Hope your son's wedding prospers.

CONTRACTED WORLD: ENLARGED VISION

Recollections of Thomas's poem "The Prisoner" may have been shadows in my mind when, in late 1993, I chose his Christmas gift—a book by a man who experienced God anew while being held captive by people who could not imagine that there was anything askew about their approach to God. The book was Terry Anderson's *Den of Lions: Memoirs of Seven Years.* Anderson, an AP correspondent in Lebanon, was seized by Shiite militants in 1985 and held until 1991. During his seven years in a cramped cell, Anderson's vision expanded. He re-embraced Catholicism and wrote poems.

These lines from Thomas's poem characterize Anderson, even if Thomas was thinking about Dietrich Bonhoeffer at the time he wrote "the Prisoner":

> 'Poems from prison! About
> what?'
>   'Life and God.' 'God
> in prison? Friend, you trifle
> with me. His face, perhaps,
> at the bars, fading
> like life.'
>
> . . . .
>
>   'It is the same
> outside. Bars, walls
> but make the perspective
> clear. *Deus absconditus!*
> We ransack the heavens,
> the distance between
> stars; the last place we look
> is in prison, his hideout
> in flesh and bone.'
>   'You believe,
> then?'
>   'The poems
> are witness. If his world
> contracted, it was to give birth
> to the larger vision. . . .'[4]

4. Thomas, *Poems of R. S. Thomas*, 102–3; "The Prisoner" ("'Poems from prison! About'").

In the spring of 1969, public television stations featured Kenneth Clark's series titled *Civilisation*. One program closed with Clark's observation that the grandiose palaces of the Papal families "were simply expressions of private greed and vanity." Then he reflected, "I wonder if a single thought that has helped forward the human spirit has ever been conceived or written down in an enormous room."[5]

When Bonhoeffer's world contracted to a Nazi prison cell, his vision expanded. He conceived and wrote down thoughts that have been reconceived and re-expressed ever since his execution nearly seven decades ago; with the result that the human spirit has been forwarded.

Bonhoeffer spent Christmas, 1943, in prison, God's "hideout / in flesh and bone." "For a Christian," Bonhoeffer wrote, "there is nothing peculiarly difficult about Christmas in a prison cell. . . . Christ was born in a stable because there was no room for him in the inn—these are things which a prisoner can understand better than anyone else."[6]

At the heart of Bonhoeffer's prison thoughts is his understanding that God is not a remote, powerful Being, who now and then drops in from outer space to rescue hapless humans from one plight or another. In Bonhoeffer's view, God is with us as a sharer of our weakness and suffering. "Man's religiosity," Bonhoeffer observed, "makes him look in his distress to the power of God in the world; he uses God as a *Deus ex machina*. The Bible however directs him to the powerlessness and suffering of God; only a suffering God can help."

Aphoristically, Bonhoeffer writes: "God allows himself to be edged out of the world and on to the cross."[7]

Hitler and his jack-booted lackeys contracted Bonhoeffer's world. Thomas contracted his own, choosing throughout his ministry to serve small parishes; opting in retirement to live in a tiny cottage. But if the worlds of Bonhoeffer and Thomas contracted, "it

5. Clark, *Civilisation*, 192.
6. Bonhoeffer, *Prisoner for God*, 59.
7. Ibid., 164.

was to give birth / to the larger vision." For Bonhoeffer, it was a vision of God present in human weakness; in the weakness of those who are confined behind bars; in the weakness of Jesus nailed to the cross. For Thomas, it was a vision of God present in the seeming absence of God; of God coming "unannounced, / remarkable merely for the absence / of clamour;" of God overflowing Thomas's life "as a chalice would / with the sea."[8]

8. Thomas, *Collected Poems 1945–1990*, 283; "Suddenly" ("As I had always known").

5

Last Visit—1994

WHILE WORKERS STRUNG UP Christmas lights outside Peterborough Cathedral, the preacher inside spoke about Abraham leaving home and trekking toward an unknown destination with nothing but faith to position himself globally.

My in-pew thoughts, obeying their own GPS, traveled toward "The Kingdom," a poem by R. S. Thomas, in which he speaks about "faith, green as a leaf." Suddenly, my attention flipped back to the preacher, who was saying something about reading a poem, which, "as the congregation would expect, is by R. S. Thomas." Then he read "The Kingdom":

> It's a long way off but inside it
> There are quite different things going on:
> Festivals at which the poor man
> Is king and the consumptive is
> Healed; mirrors in which the blind look
> At themselves and love looks at them
> Back; and industry is for mending
> The bent bones and the minds fractured
> By life. It's a long way off, but to get
> There takes no time and admission
> Is free, if you will purge yourself
> Of desire, and present yourself with
> Your need only and the simple offering
> Of your faith, green as a leaf.[1]

1. Thomas, *Collected Poems* 1945–1990, 233; "The Kingdom" ("It's a long

After the service, I greeted the preacher and said, "My wife and I are planning to spend three days this week with Thomas." "But," he sputtered, "he's a recluse!"

Two days later, I called the "recluse" from the hotel room he had reserved for Nancy and me. "I'll collect you tomorrow at two o'clock," he said, "take you to Bangor and show you my university college." The next few days were the richest of my three visits, but I almost scuttled the experience by forgetting that would-be biographers brought out Thomas's face of stone.

From "R. S." to "Ronald"

Ten months earlier, I had received a postcard from Thomas thanking me for my Christmas gift, *Den of Lions: Memoirs of Seven Years* by Terry A. Anderson, the AP correspondent in Lebanon, who, as we saw in the last chapter, was seized by Shiite militants in 1985. Thomas wrote:

> Y Rhiw, Pwllheli, Cymru (Wales)
> January 14, 1994
> [no salutation]
>
> It was kind of you to send the book which I read with admiration. A successful 1994 to you both.
>
> R. S.

Responding in mid February, I told him that friends had invited Nancy and me to join them at Cambridge University in November. From there, I said, "Nancy and I would like to drive to Aberdaron to visit you. Perhaps you would be willing to set aside several days to be with us." He replied shortly after his eighty-first birthday:

---

way off but inside it").

A Masterwork of Doubting-Belief

Y Rhiw, Pwllheli, Cymru (Wales)
March 31, 1994

Dear John

Thank you for your birthday greetings. I am writing this from my friends' home, but intend returning to mine on Easter Monday. My 6 months stint is at an end. I have not done much solid reading, but have passed the mornings in writing poetry. I don't think it is of any significance. I have shot my bolt at last. Plenty of interesting ideas, but, as Mallarmé remarked, poetry is not made with ideas.

I hope your plans for your book are progressing. As far as I know now, I will be at Rhiw in November and pleased to see you.

With kind wishes
R. S.

Thomas, in a letter to Raymond Garlick, said he had taken Upper House at Presteigne "for 6 months to be near some friends who have problems." He had met them, Betty Vernon and her daughter, Alice, when they lived in Eglwys-fach.[2]

My next letter to Thomas expressed doubts about whether he had shot his bolt; in fact, however, the last book of new poems published during his lifetime, *No Truce with the Furies*, came out in 1995, which means that most of the poems were written before 1994. Also in my letter I offered several November dates for my proposed visit, and reported that my book proposal, "R. S. Thomas: The Poet for Pastors," remained in the hands of a publisher. Thomas, replying, switched from "I" to "we." This seemed significant, since he was not prone to using the editorial, or, heaven forbid! the royal, "we":

2. Davies, *Thomas: Letters to Garlick*, 147, 148.

Y Rhiw, Pwllheli, Cymru
May 7, 1994

Dear John

Thank you for your letter. We shall be pleased to see you both.

I suggest Tuesday Nov. 8th because the earlier the better. It can turn very wet as autumn sets in.

We are in residence now, but there has been a lot to do after 6 months absence. The mice especially enjoyed themselves.

Yours sincerely
R. S.

It was good to have a firm date. But who had changed Thomas's "I" to "we"? In his next letter, he switched back to "I":

Cefn Du Ganol, Llanfairynghornwy, Holyhead.
Gwynedd
July 8, 1994

Dear John

Thank you for your last letter. I can't remember if there is anything else I should thank you for, as things have been in a muddle lately. You will see from the above address that I am now living in Ynys Môn (Anglesey). I don't know how this will affect your projected visit in November. I am about 70 miles from Aberdaron, but only about 12 from Caergybi (Holyhead) up in the north west corner of Anglesey and about 22 from Bangor. Let me know if you would prefer to cancel Carreg Plas and let me find you somewhere in Anglesey.

Things were getting beyond me at Rhiw – too much work cutting hedges, grass and generally keeping nature at bay. Ynys Môn has always been good for birds and there is a sanctuary near here.

With best wishes
R. S.

Responding as soon as I received his letter, I said that I had cancelled my Carreg Plas booking, welcomed his offer to find a hotel for Nancy and me in Anglesey, and asked if he had received the two books by Loren Eiseley that I sent. Thomas used both "I" and "we" in his reply:

> Cefn Du Ganol, Llanfairynghornwy, Holyhead.
> Gwynedd LL65 4LG
> August 12, 1994
>
> Dear John
>
> Thank you for your letter. Yes, I did receive the 2 books and apologize for not acknowledging them sooner.
>
> The cruise we went on was not aimed at birds, so I didn't see many. Mainly I had an overdose of scenery. As Wallace Stevens said: 'Panoramas are not what they used to be'.
>
> I have booked you in at a hotel about 6 miles up the coast from here, near Amlwch, for the nights of 8, 9, 10, 11 in November. I take it that a double bedroom en suite is what you require.
>
> We shall look forward. I will send directions nearer the time.
>
> Greetings
> R. S.

During a conversation three months later, Thomas remarked that "we" flew from Heathrow to Seattle, where they boarded a ship for a cruise to Alaska. He expected, he said, to see new birds when they went ashore, but was disappointed. Yet later in the evening he reported that he had seen about thirty new species, including the bald eagle.

When I responded to his letter, I thanked him for the hotel booking, then said that my poetry bookseller in Hay-on-Wye had written that a rumor was going around that Thomas had married. "If it is true, Nancy joins me in sending heartiest best wishes to you and your wife. If it is not true, please excuse my impertinence." Finally, I told him that the editor I was working with on my Thomas project called and said she expected little difficulty with the editorial committee, while anticipating rough sailing with the marketing crew.

Responding, he said nothing about the marriage rumor, but did, for the first time, sign himself "Ronald":

> Cefn Du Ganol, Llanfairynghornwy, Holyhead.
> Gwynedd LL65 4LG
> October 6, 1994
>
> Dear John
>
> Thank you for your last letter. As I said I have booked a double room at the Bull Bay Hotel from 8th–12th November.
>
> The telephone number is 0407 830 223.
>
> Your best way by car would be, having crossed either of the bridges into Anglesey, to turn right for the Amlwch road round the coast, A 5025. Bull Bay—Porth Llechog in Welsh, is about 2 miles beyond Amlwch. You can then telephone here at your convenience on 730 943. I hope you arrive safely and find the place easily.
>
> Yours sincerely
> Ronald

Meanwhile I had done something that threatened to scuttle the newfound "Ronald" relationship. The day before Thomas wrote that letter, I sent a package containing the research material I had gathered. "As you page through it," I wrote, "you will note the questions I would like to discuss. Perhaps there will be inquiries you would prefer not to deal with. If so, mark them and simply tell me 'to move on' when we get to them."

Thomas's reply bore the imprint of his face of stone. The letter was typed, except for "Dear John" at the beginning and "Yours sincerely, Ronald" at the close. It arrived the day Nancy and I were scheduled to fly to London.

A Masterwork of Doubting-Belief

> Cefn Du Ganol, Llanfairynghornwy, Holyhead.
> Gwynedd LL65 4LG
> October 27, 1994
>
> Dear John
>
> I have been looking at your proposed scheme of work, which you sent me, and I think I ought to let you know before you arrive that I would not be prepared to co-operate in the more personal aspects of your study. I had thought that you were undertaking a study of my work and not a biography. I have never answered question-naires and have refused to co-operate with intending bi-ographers. I would consider showing you such trivialities as where I lived in Caergybi or what hostels I occupied as a student as entirely irrelevant to my poetry.
>
> I would agree that some of my poetry has a very personal element and I would have to discuss this where it might be of any help in elucidating the poetry itself. But details about my mother's maiden name and what she died of appear to me to have nothing to do with the poetry.
>
> In the circumstances, if you still think it worth your while coming all this way, I shall expect to hear from you after you have settled into the hotel.
>
> Yours sincerely
> Ronald

My nervous system went into high-caffeine mode, but some-how I composed and typed a reply. After taking it to the post office, I dialed his number. He answered, and I apologized, repeating more or less what I had written:

> I have no intention of writing a biography. Rather, I did the research I sent you as a way for me of coming to understand your poetry better. And for me, under-standing always involves seeing—seeing Wales, seeing the places you have seen. That was the reason I visited Manafon, Eglwys-fach, and Aberdaron in 1992. That is why I would like to visit Caergybi and Bangor this time.

But all this 'seeing' is merely to aid in understanding. My
book proposal remains what it has always been—a book
to present your poetry to American pastors.

In my research, I was carried away by my historian's
training, which taught me to ask questions. All these
questions can be ignored. As I said in my letter of October 5, you can simply tell me 'to move on.'

Thomas accepted my apology and agreed to proceed with my
visit. So I was somewhat calmer when, seven hours after opening his letter, Nancy and I boarded our flight from Philadelphia
to London. A week later, the day after the Peterborough preacher
called Thomas "a recluse," we stopped at Llandudno, a resort on the
north coast of Wales. Walking along the rain-swept promenade, I
noticed something scrawled in black marker on the glass screen at
the bandstand. "Rage," it said, "against the machine." Has Thomas,
I wondered, turned graffitist?

Thomas used *machine* to symbolize all aspects of technology.
In a poem published in *Counterpoint*, a book he urged me to read,
he provides a script for the machine:

> 'The body is mine and the soul is mine'
> says the machine. 'I am at the dark source
> where the good is indistinguishable
> from evil. I fill my tanks up
> and there is war. I empty them
> and there is not peace. . . .'[3]

Leaving Llandudno, with its Thomasian graffito "Rage
against the machine," I drove across one of the Menai Strait bridges
and headed counterclockwise around Anglesey to Bull Bay. After
checking in at "the most northerly hotel in Wales," I called Thomas,
who said he would "collect" Nancy and me at two o'clock the next
afternoon for a trip to Bangor.

The evening newsreader on BBC announced that "all indica-
tions point to a massive repudiation of President Clinton." It was

3. Thomas, *Collected Later Poems* 1988–2000, 115; "'The body is mine and
the soul is mine.'"

Tuesday, November 8, 1994. The next morning, BBC reported "a Republican sweep," an "earthquake," in the congressional elections. Later in the day, Thomas called recent U.S. presidents a "succession of duds."

"We Welsh Have Given Enough Blood to the English"

Several hours before his "duds" remark, Thomas arrived at the Bull Bay Hotel driving his white VW hatchback. His hair was longer than last year, with a crisp curliness. Although Nancy and I were bundled up against the November chill, he seemed comfortable wearing a sports jacket, blue shirt with red stripes, red necktie, and red suspenders.

As we drove across the Menai Strait bridge from Anglesey to Bangor, Thomas mentioned violence in the United States, and the knives used for murders in Britain; he favored a ban on knives. Remembering an invitation to be poet in residence at Amherst College, he said he turned it down, because he did not take to New England winters.

Finding a parking spot in Bangor, he showed us the church hostel where he lived as a "theolog" studying classics at the University College. In the hostel's chapel, with its lingering aroma of incense, Thomas revealed that daily high church worship was an important part of his spiritual formation.

We walked on to the original buildings of the University College, which he liked, but called the modern buildings "excrescences." The classics department in his day emphasized Latin, not Greek, authors. "I never cared for the Romans," he said; "I much preferred the Greeks." Later, he put classics aside to concentrate on learning Welsh—a decision he now "regretted."

That "regretted" shattered an image. The poet, who was seen by many as a self-certified inspector of pure Welshness, rued having put Latin and Greek literature aside in favor of Welsh.

Only minutes later, as we were leaving a university building, he spied a sign in English urging students to "Give Blood," and snarled, "We Welsh have given enough blood to the English." At our next stop, St. Deiniol's Cathedral, he grumbled about the English labels on various items. When I pointed to some with Welsh signs, he termed them "afterthoughts."

It became clear to me as we drove from Bangor back to Bull Bay that Thomas had timed our afternoon to ensure that we returned to the Anglesey side of the Menai Strait as the setting sun was illuminating the autumn-colored hillsides on the opposite shore, above which loomed the cloud-hidden mountains of Snowdonia. It was as if he were saying, "I have allowed you to see 'such trivialities' as the church hostel where I lived and the building where I attended lectures in classics. Now I want you to see what is essential to my being: the Welsh landscape, whose 'colours / Are renewed daily with variations / Of light and distance that no painter / Achieves or suggests.'"[4]

Parking briefly in front of Beaumaris Castle, he got in digs at the English and us Americans. "The castle," he said, "was built by Edward I to keep the Welsh in line." "Americans," he added, "seem to like castles." It was spoken in a tone to indicate that castles were not for him, at least not English castles that the Welsh had not captured. In an early poem, he refers to Wales having neither present nor future, "only the past, / Brittle with relics, / Wind-bitten towers and castles / With sham ghosts."[5]

Continuing our drive, Thomas remarked that his son made the selections for *Collected Poems* 1945–1990, which was published in 1993. He would "have chosen differently," he said. He got out of the car to say goodbye to us at the hotel, noted that he would be back at 1:30 the next day, and said he and his "friend" were inviting us to supper in the evening.

Thomas and I talked for more than two hours the following afternoon. It was a semiformal interview: I had a list of questions, and scribbled down his responses, but there was no tape recorder. Later, he took Nancy and me for a short drive under a lowering sky

4. Thomas, *Collected Poems* 1945–1990, 81; "The View from the Window" ("Like a painting it is set before one").

5. Ibid. 37; "Welsh Landscape" ("To live in Wales is to be conscious").

to point out an old stone windmill and a small army of modern electricity-generating wind turbines. They are preferable, he said, to the nuclear power station visible from his cottage, but he wished they were sited so as not "to damage the natural beauty." Also he expressed disdain for "the pylons marching across Anglesey to deliver power to England."

During the drive, Thomas explained why he moved from his cottage at Y Rhiw to his present cottage, Cefn Du Ganol. "There was too much grass to keep down, too many hedges to cut," and there was no bus service for "when my doctor tells me I can no longer drive." So when he met an artist from Anglesey, he asked him to keep him in mind if a cottage became available on Anglesey. "Three months later, the artist rang and told me about Cefn Du Ganol, which is located on a ridge that I could see from my childhood home."

Back at the hotel, he drew a map to help me find his cottage in the dense November darkness. A few hours later, as Nancy and I approached Cefn Du Ganol, Thomas was coming down the driveway waving a flashlight that he used to direct us to a parking spot, then to light our way into his home. Outdoor electric lights were anathema: He refused to allow anything artificial to blur his view of "the sleepless conurbations / of the stars."[6]

"English Women Drink Pink Gin; English Men, Whiskey"

Entering Thomas's cottage, I was immediately struck by the difference between it and his home at Y Rhiw. Clearly a woman was in residence, a woman who possessed an eye for room arrangement comparable to his eye for word placement. The colors in the fabric on the sofa rhymed with the colors of the books on the shelves, and a rhythm moved between the shimmering silver on the mantle and a bouquet of bronze-colored bracken on a side table.

Then the woman who composed the room appeared. "My friend," Thomas said, "Betty Vernon." Soon we were seated close

6. Ibid., 296; "Alive" ("It is alive. It is you").

to one another in front of a wood fire that Thomas occasionally poked into brighter, warmer life.

"Drinks?" Betty wondered, assuring us that "English women drink pink gin; English men, whiskey."

Another Thomasian paradox: In the home of the prince of Welshness, Nancy and I received guidance about the favorite drinks of English women and men.

Nancy passed on the pink gin, opting rather to join Ronald who, preferring sweet wine, asked for cream sherry. I played Englishman. Betty sipped pink gin and smoked a cigarillo.

Betty's extroversion balanced Ronald's introversion. We touched on American politics, health care, the Native Americans. When Betty went to the kitchen, Ronald mentioned that he gave his copies of his early books to his son to prepare *Collected Poems 1945–1990*. I'm "not sure," he said, "where they are now."

He recalled his offer to retire as vicar of the parish of St. Hywyn, Aberdaron, but continue, without salary, to serve the parish for the privilege of continuing to live in the vicarage. The "bishop dithered," so Thomas gave notice of his intention to retire. It took the bishop fifteen years to appoint a new vicar, and "he's a mess— can't preach in Welsh."

Betty's dinner provided a taste of Wales: Welsh lamb with mint sauce and currant jelly, roasted potatoes with gravy, leeks, and tomatoes cooked together. Ronald cleared the table, then served slices of orange with cream, followed by cheese from England and France: Double Gloucester and Bleu.

Our table talk centered on church life in America—women clergy, even women bishops. Betty opposed them, not liking their preaching voices; Ronald, she said, felt less strongly. He said nothing. The American system of paying janitors to clean the church shocked her. Back in her home parish, she and other women cleaned the church, even though they had full-time servants or hired cleaners to skivvy in their own homes.

Ronald complained about public address systems. When he was speaking at the memorial service for Vernon Watkins, "they hung this thing around my neck and told me to speak in a normal voice. I did so, and no one could hear me—they forgot to turn the machine on."

Back at the fireside, Betty poured demitasses of coffee and handed round a bowl of chocolates. We talked about church music. Ronald mentioned that the organist at Manafon, his first parish, was a woman who "ruined every service." Also he pointed to a defect in the training at his theological college: It's failure to teach candidates for ordination to read music and lead congregational singing.

As we were getting ready to leave, Betty expressed the hope that the days ahead would be sunny, then added, "Of course, God sometimes sends rain." "No," Ronald parried, "he doesn't." Even in small talk, he refused to countenance theological sloppiness. God does not sit at a celestial control panel, deciding when and where to open the rain sluices. God created a world in which the laws of meteorology govern the weather.

Under cloudy skies the next afternoon, Thomas drove Nancy and me to the seaport where he grew up, Caergybi (Holyhead), and showed us more "trivialities": the ferry docks from which his father sailed as an officer on the Irish Sea ferries. The English-speaking church that Thomas and his mother attended has been torn down, as has his school. We went on to Holyhead Mountain and looked at round stone huts that date to a thousand years before the birth of Jesus. On to the lighthouse at South Stack, where migratory birds stop in large numbers; only the resident seagulls were there. Then Thomas pointed out the house of boyhood friends and the cove with a beach where he and the friends went swimming.

Three weeks earlier, Thomas had written, as we recall, that he "would consider showing [me] such trivialities as where I lived in Caergybi or what hostels I occupied as a student as entirely irrelevant to my poetry." Yet he had just devoted, over the course of three days, more than six hours to showing me such places, and "the recluse" had allowed me to interview him for more than two hours and to share table talk for another six.

Ronald and Betty were our guests for dinner at the Bull Bay Hotel on our last evening there. We talked about poetry, and he said he thought "interest in poetry is waning and poetry will disappear." I countered, saying, "If I may quote: 'Why so fast, / mortal?'"—the question God asks Thomas when he concludes that "Religion is over."[7] Betty smiled; a twinkle appeared in Ronald's eye. When I said that the preacher at Peterborough Cathedral had called him a "recluse," Betty said, "He *is* something of a recluse." Ronald added that when the English started buying Welsh cottages, he refused to do poetry readings in England, which "may have given me a reclusive cast." At dessert time, Ronald grinned, "Do you think they'll have ice cream?" Face of flesh hyphenated with face of stone.

We moved into the residents' lounge, where Thomas said he planned to stop reading his poems publicly after January 1, 1995, but would do a private reading for a small tour I was leading the following summer. Betty asked about our next stops. Picking up on our plan to visit to Hay-on-Wye, she urged us to try the Rhydspence Inn.

When Thomas brought the car to the hotel door for Betty, we said goodbye to one another. Although we corresponded for the next six years, I never saw him again.

A Krystallnacht Sort of Fascist

Dinnertime the next evening found Nancy and me back at the Maybank Hotel in Aberdyfi, where Thomas had joined us the previous year. This year, as it turned out, we were there for roast Thomas, even though roast lamb was on our plates. The Maybank was closed for the month of November, but the English co-owners, Liz and Paul, opened a room for us and invited a Welsh couple, Madeline and Jim, to be part of a private dinner party. Jim was born in the coal-mining valleys of South Wales, but went to Cambridge University and taught biology in the London area until, retiring, he and Madeline returned to Wales. Since the English had welcomed him when he went to England to study and teach, he deplored Thomas's opposition to English buyers of Welsh cottages.

7. Ibid., 282; "The Moon in Lleyn" ("The last quarter of the moon").

He lambasted Thomas's acceptance, if not encouragement, of the arson campaign against English-owned holiday properties.

To cap his fury, Jim called Thomas a Krystallnacht sort of fascist. Just as Nazis shattered the windows of Jewish synagogues, homes, and shops to frighten Jews into leaving Germany, so Thomas, in Jim's view, was a fascist in his willingness to countenance the use of arson to scare off English men and women who wanted to "live," in Thomas's words, "cheap off dear things" of Wales.[8]

Jim's fascist label for Thomas was picked up, minus the rancor, by Richard Spencer at the next stop Nancy and I made. Spencer was the New Testament tutor at Saint Michael's College, Llandaff, a suburb of Cardiff, the theological college where Thomas spent a year preparing for ordination. The fascist label, Spencer said, was pinned on Thomas by Welsh people who resented Thomas's self-crowning as the prince of pure Welshness. His articulation of the Welsh Nationalist cause, Spencer continued, was not shared by the majority of the Welsh, who wrote him off as a fussy purist, ranting about the borrowing of English words to fill in the gaps in the Welsh language.

Spencer thought that fuming about Thomas's self-appointed guardianship of the Welsh language prevented people from recognizing and celebrating one of his major accomplishments: putting English-language poetry on a strict diet. Spencer said that Thomas was "ascetic" in his poetry, writing short poems with lean words and succinct titles.

"What," I asked Spencer, as our conversation over lunch continued, "was the greatest contribution of Saint Michael's College to Thomas?" The school's "high church views," he answered, which prevailed in the 1930s. Spencer explained that the college had been founded by Welsh Anglicans who emphasized awe in the presence of the Almighty, traditional Eucharist-centered liturgies, and the role of the priest as the intermediary between his congregants and God. Thomas shunned the "smells and bells," the colorful vestments, and richly appointed churches so often associated

---

8. Thomas, *Collected Later Poems* 1988–2000, 34; "And this one with his starched lip."

with high church Anglicanism, terming them "the confections / Of worship."[9] But he insisted that awe is the proper stance of the worshiper, adhered to Eucharist-centered liturgies, and refused to budge from the traditional place of the priest when celebrating the Eucharist. He understood his role, he told me, as the intermediary between the congregation and God—facing the altar, his back to the congregation, leading his parishioners up into the presence of *I Am Who I Am.*

My next interview at St. Michael's was with John Rowlands, the college's head, who understood Thomas as a John the Baptist crying in the wilderness, trying to point people to a theology that is open to the discoveries of science and to the angst of contemporary women and men. Thomas, Rowlands said, "is a prophetic figure, one we need to hear," but who is not without honor except in his own country. Using Henry II's words with regard to Archbishop Thomas Becket, Rowlands said the Welsh attitude towards Thomas was, "Who will rid us of this turbulent priest?" The Church in Wales, Rowlands continued, sees Thomas as eccentric and pessimistic, as a doom-and-gloom writer, but, Rowlands asserted, Thomas "will be read for years to come." And even now his poetry is included in the standard high school exam.

For many persons today, Rowlands concluded, Thomas speaks an unknown language, and tries to make himself heard where "machinery" is turning "All to noise."[10] Yet voices crying in the wilderness do, if they are of God, eventually gain a hearing.

"THEY'RE DEARS"

Nancy and I made our final 1994 Thomas-related stop at the fourteenth-century Rhydspence Inn, which is near Hay-on-Wye, on the English side of a sign that says "Welcome to Wales." In the bar before dinner, I mentioned to the English owners, Pam and Peter Glover, that Betty Vernon had recommended their inn. Pam

9. Thomas, *Collected Poems* 1945–1990, 187; "Sir Gelli Meurig" ("I imagine it, a land").

10. Ibid., 178; "The Face" ("When I close my eyes, I can see it").

became voluble: "They're dears," referring to Betty and R. S. They often come here for lunch, she went on, from Betty's home in Titley, and sometimes they stay overnight, always in room one, which she proceeded to show us.

Straight off, Pam continued, when R. S. and Betty arrive at the inn, Betty asks for a pink gin. Once R. S. kidded her when she ordered French fries with salmon. On another occasion, when Peter was giving Pam money to buy a posh frock to go to a dance at her son's school, Betty told Peter to give Pam more money; she needed to get a really nice dress. When they are leaving, Pam noted, Betty urges R. S. to give Pam a kiss, which he does reluctantly, shy and embarrassed.

One more Thomasian paradox: It was necessary to cross over into England to find appreciation for Thomas's face of flesh; in Wales, he was a stone-faced fascist.

6

"A Religious Poet Struggling to Identify God in an Age of Science and Technology"

THE FIRST FIVE CHAPTERS of this book introduced R. S. Thomas as a man of hyphenated identities.

In chapter 1, we saw him living in the tension between his Cymric and Anglo heritages and between his birth language, English, and his acquired language, Welsh. Also we identified his natural habitat—a peninsula, a land-sea-sky location. Finally, I suggested that it was harder than Thomas admitted for him to harness together his two callings: the calling of God to be an Anglican priest and the calling of Euterpe to be a lyric poet.

Chapter 2 presented Thomas as a doubting-believer, and it examined the doubting-believer's God, the elusive *I Will Be Who I Will Be*[1] of the Bible. Chapters 3, 4, and 5 revealed the Ronald I learned to know: a personable, caring, even funny man—the face of flesh in contrast with the public view of him as a face of stone.

This chapter and the next single out the philosophers, theologians, and poets whose writings influenced Thomas's thinking.

---

1. Exod 3:14.

A Masterwork of Doubting-Belief

Stocking the Shelves of the Mind

"How," I asked Thomas, as the glowing bars of an electric fire pushed back the November chill, "do you stock the shelves of your mind? What authors have you read?"

He answered, as I interviewed him in the lounge of the Bull Bay Hotel, that he was not a student, at least not in the sense of someone who, when reading a book, underscores sentences, takes notes, and prepares outlines. "You can't expect," he continued, "my kind of poet to be as learned as non-creative people, who may spend a morning doing research and amassing a considerable amount of information. On the other hand, while I did spend time reading and studying, I would often devote the better part of a morning to the writing of a poem."

"The scholarly // mind gives a dry light,"[2] Thomas observes. "Poetry is that / which arrives at the intellect / by way of the heart."[3]

Unamuno, Yeats, and Shelley

Continuing to reflect on the stocking of his mind, Thomas said, "I catch the odd idea as it goes by and incorporate it in a poem and thereby give the impression of being well up on this and that."

Pursuing the sources of his ideas, I asked, "What did the reading of classics at Bangor mean to you?" "It would have been better for me," he answered, "to have taken a degree in English rather than classics. Nevertheless, my training in classics served me as a poet in the sense that one who translates is constantly involved in the search for the right word to construe the original. Therefore reading classics was a good discipline for me as a budding poet."

"Did you," I wondered, "pick up your tragic sense of life from the Greeks, from the tragedies of the Greek dramatists?" "I see," Thomas answered, "my tragic sense of life—your phrase, John, not mine—as owing less to the Greeks, as you suggested, than to

2. Thomas, *Collected Later Poems* 1988–2000, 327; "Class" ("The professor lectures upon Blake").

3. Ibid., 355; "Don't ask me."

Unamuno, to the lines Yeats wrote for his tombstone, and to Shelley's 'Ozymandias.'"

In Shelley's poem, a traveler spies two gigantic stone legs standing in the desert, while nearby the statue's head lies half buried in the sand, its "shattered visage" still projecting a "sneer of cold command."

> And on the pedestal these words appear:
> 'My name is Ozymandias, king of kings:
> Look on my works, ye Mighty, and despair!'
> Nothing beside remains. Round the decay
> Of that colossal wreck, boundless and bare
> The lone and level sands stretch far away.

The words chiseled into Yeats's gravestone address persons who happen to pass by, riders with their knee-boots planted firmly, perhaps haughtily, in the stirrups. Yeats admonishes them to view life and death with a well-iced eye. He counsels acceptance of the fact that death is as natural as life; that we did not ask for the one and cannot evade the other. Therefore we are to gaze at living and dying dispassionately, with studied indifference.

Adhering to Yeats's icy view of life, Thomas writes: "I am eyes / Merely, . . seeing the young born / Fair, knowing the cancer / Awaits them."[4]

Miguel de Unamuno (1864–1936), the third person Thomas mentioned in response to my question about his tragic sense of life, was a Spanish philosopher, poet, and professor of Greek. In his book *The Tragic Sense of Life*—which, Thomas told me, "appealed to [his] romanticism"—Unamuno acknowledges that the scientific and poetic viewpoints cannot be reconciled. Each will always find fault with the other. But that antagonism must not be used as an excuse for an exclusive adoption of one perspective or the other.

Unamuno never closed himself off from either Scripture or science. He refused to bar his mind to the findings of science that call God into question. Likewise, he refused to shut down his brain to believers' experiences of the presence of God. He acknowledged,

---

4. Thomas, *Collected Poems* 1945–1990, 209; "Petition" ("And I standing in the shade").

however, that his two great refusals were irreconcilable. There is no rational way to heal the cleavage between the reasons of the head and the reasons of the heart. So a life truly lived is sustained, in Thomas's phrase, by the "ability // to hold all things in play."[5]

Two quotations capture Unamuno's position:

> . . . the most tragic problem of philosophy is to reconcile intellectual necessities with the necessities of the heart and the will.[6]

> Those who believe that they believe in God, but without any passion in their heart, without anguish of mind, without uncertainty, without doubt, without an element of despair even in their consolation, believe only in the God-idea, not in God Himself.[7]

Thomas believed in God, not the God-idea. He believed with passion in his heart, with anguish of mind, with uncertainty, with doubt, with an element of despair. He was passionately engaged with a God who eluded his understanding, who remained elusive even in self-revelation.

"I Lacked Someone to Guide My Poetic Development"

We have identified thinkers who influenced what I have called Thomas's tragic sense of life. Next we'll consider poets who played a role in his evolution as a poet.

Because I remembered reading that Palgrave's anthology of poetry, *The Golden Treasury*, had influenced Thomas, I asked: "What appealed to you in Palgrave's *Golden Treasury*?" He answered: "The *Golden Treasury* was all I had. I lacked someone to guide my poetic development. So I did not realize Palgrave was forty years behind the times. It does, however, contain some gems

5. Thomas, *Collected Later Poems 1988–2000*, 206; "Sonata in X" ("What's that you've got on?").

6. Unamuno, *Tragic Sense of Life*, 15.

7. Ibid., 193.

of English poetry, even though it had not come to terms with Hopkins and Yeats."

When Thomas could have been learning from Hopkins and Yeats, from Eliot, Joyce, and Pound, his tutors were the poets selected by Palgrave, an anthologist stuck in the nineteenth century; whose *Golden Treasury* was first published in 1861. And for Thomas, a lover of the open air, the nature poetry of Hardy would have been appealing as well as instructive. But all he had was Shelley's weaker work.

Thomas did, of course, begin to read the major poets of his times, but he has left it to his readers to determine the particular ones that interested him and how, if at all, they influenced his style. All he told me was that he "began to read Manley Hopkins, Yeats, and Eliot." Nothing more was mentioned about the latter two, but he elaborated on Hopkins.

"I wouldn't say that Manley Hopkins influenced me; certainly not his rhythms. More appealing to me than his 'terrible' sonnets were his two 'wreck' poems—'The Wreck of the Deutschland' and 'The Loss of the Eurydice.'" Remembering the way that God in Thomas's poems is occasionally, suddenly, an enlivening presence, it may be that Thomas was taken by a line in the first 'wreck' poem: "Let him easter in us, be a dayspring to the dimness of us."[8]

Thomas went on to say that he particularly liked "the last line of one 'terrible' sonnet, where Hopkins, who has been struggling with someone he addresses as "O thou terrible," concludes:

> That night, that year
> Of now done darkness I wretch lay wrestling with (my God!)
> my God.[9]

Moving on, I asked: "Does the poetic muse need a person of the borders through whom to speak—in your case, the borders between England and Wales, between the English and Welsh languages, between the land and the sea, between the earth and the

8. Gardner, *Poems of Gerard Manley Hopkins*, 63; "The Wreck of the Deutschland."

9. Ibid., 100; Sonnet 64, "Carrion Comfort."

sky?" Thomas interjected: "Between belief and unbelief. Tensions are endless."

In his preface to the *Penguin Book of Religious Verse*, Thomas says, quoting Keats, that "Poetry is born of the tensions set up by the poet's ability to be 'in uncertainties, mysteries, doubts, without any irritable reaching after fact and reason.'"[10] Poets are not fundamentalists, whether of the religious or the scientific variety. They do not demand tidy answers to every question, neat solutions to every problem. Poets who are religious worship a mysterious God—*I Am Who I Am*. Those who are not religious respond to a mysterious muse.

Among other tensions, Thomas explored those between his attitude toward God and George Herbert's; also between his and that of Welsh poet Edward Thomas, who said "that God is "stone-deaf and stone- / blind."[11]

"I would not use that statement," R. S. observed, "but I do insist that God's thoughts are not our thoughts."

God is not so aloof that a relationship between humans and God is impossible, but God is so wondrous, so awe-inspiring, that coziness is inappropriate. For that reason, Thomas said: "I have lost my ability to read George Herbert. Herbert's God is not my God. I cannot get on matey terms with the deity as Herbert can."

SPENGLER, ORTEGA, BERDYAEV, AND BERGSON

Speaking further about writers who influenced his thinking, Thomas said: "A poet is a parasite: He seizes on ideas and gives the impression of being well read, of being an authority." Then he named Spengler, Ortega y Gasset, Berdyaev, and Bergson as authors who influenced his thinking.

Oswald Spengler (1880–1936), a German historian and philosopher, delved into science, mathematics, and art, as well as philosophy and history. In his best-known work, *The Decline of the*

---

10. Thomas, *Penguin Book of Religious Verse*, 11.

11. Thomas, Edward, *Collected Poems*, 108; "February Afternoon."

West, he argues that civilizations rise and fall in cycles, with Western civilization now being in a period of decay. "I was influenced," Thomas told me, "by Spengler's *Decline of the West*. The decline of the West, I think, is an ongoing concept," which "appealed, I suppose, to my romanticism."

José Ortega y Gasset (1883–1955), along with Unamuno, belonged to the Generation of '98, Spanish intellectuals who grappled with Spain's decline as a world power, which, beginning in the seventeenth century, reached its low point in 1898, when Spain lost her last colonies in the Caribbean and the Pacific. Among the other members of the Generation of '98 are such poets, artists, and composers as García Lorca, Picasso, and Granados. Responding to their country's diminishment as an empire, they sought to define the essential, abiding quality of Spain, which is what Thomas strove to do for Wales, a nation diminished, as he saw it, by centuries of English political dominance and cultural arrogance.

The writings of Ortega range over history, politics, art criticism, metaphysics, and ethics. Influenced by Spengler's *Decline of the West*, Ortega focuses on the decay of civilization in Spain, believing that democracy's enthronement of majority opinion was producing a culture lacking in vitality and vision.

Ortega's philosophy was existentialist, as was that of Unamuno and Nikolai Berdyaev (1874–1948), whose form of existentialism was rooted in Russian Orthodoxy. One description of Berdyaev's thinking sounds like the theology found in Thomas's poetry:

> [God] may be known only in the existential encounter, in the "I-Thou" relationship which is primarily that of communion rather than of intellectual apprehension. For spirit with Spirit can meet. Our knowledge of God is, therefore, basically intuitive, subjective, experiential. . . . It is neither exclusively intellectual, emotional, volitional, nor intuitional, but rather integral, combining all these four together . . .[12]

---

12. Michalson, *Christianity and the Existentialists*, 63.

When you are talking with a person, you do not debate her existence; you simply share a conversation. You experience an I-to-I meeting. Similarly, our relationship with God is either an encounter of the *human* "I" and the *divine* "I", or it is nothing. Debates about the existence or non-existence of God are futile.

Henri Bergson (1859–1941), a French philosopher, received the Nobel Prize in Literature in 1927. In his book *Creative Evolution*, he says that science views life as a current flowing inexorably toward death and nothingness. There is, however, a counter current, that of the human spirit, the *élan vital*, vigorously flowing backward against the flow toward nothingness. This countering *élan* is *vital*. It affirms life in the flow toward death; creates dams of meaning in currents of meaninglessness.

Thomas, during my interview with him, said that we "must come to terms with this question: To what extent can we say 'God' in response to modern science?" Later, he added: "I believe there is a movement in England to keep me viewed as a country poet. Much more, I am a religious poet struggling to identify God in an age of science and technology."

Although Thomas never named the philosophical underpinning of his struggle, it is clear from the writers he cited as influencing his thinking and from his own poems about God, science, and "The cold brain of the machine / That will destroy you,"[13] that his theology was informed by the existentialist tradition. Within this tradition, affirmations of God are leaps of faith. Their model is the disciple Peter, who, when he saw Jesus walked toward him on the sea, "got out of the boat, started walking on the water, and came toward Jesus."[14]

THOMAS: A POET IN THE EXISTENTIALIST TRADITION

People who think and write in the existentialist tradition know that the meaning of life and death cannot be read off of the world's

13. Thomas, *Collected Poems 1945–1990*, 108; "Too Late" ("I would have spared you this, Prytherch").

14. Matt 14:29

natural facts. Some facts point to a good God; some to a bad. We see, in Thomas's words, "the young born / Fair, knowing the cancer / Awaits them."[15]

Existentialists recognize that the existence of God cannot be established by an analysis of the design of the cosmos, by considering how everything seems to be part of a plan. To be sure, there are aspects of the natural world that make it not unreasonable, not irrational, to believe in God. But this belief is not something that can be subjected to scientific scrutiny, to objective proof.

Our knowledge of God is not intellectual; it is existential. It responds to the heart's reasons, not the mind's reasoning. It is "basically intuitive, subjective, experiential. . . . It is neither exclusively intellectual, emotional, volitional, nor intuitional, but rather integral, combining all these four together."

Thomas uses an existentialist approach to identifying God in an age when science and technology raise doubts in many minds about God. He launches himself toward God across fathoms of uncertainty, doubt, and unbelief. Some of these launches result in experiences of God's absence; others, however, lead to experiences of the sustaining presence of God.

But even Thomas's experiences of God's presence do not produce mind-satisfying answers to questions about why we live in a world where we see "the young born / Fair, knowing the cancer / Awaits them."

Thomas believed in God existentially, with passion in his heart, with anguish of mind aroused by the world's two-sidedness, with doubt elicited by science and everyday experience, with an element of despair. But always with the hope, the expectation, that the emptiness of his life without God was a vacuum that *I Am*, suddenly, would fill.

---

15. Thomas, *Collected Poems 1945–1990*, 209; "Petition" ("And I standing in the shade").

Kierkegaard and Tillich

Thomas, after saying, "I've caught the odd idea from Ortega, Berdyaev, and Kierkegaard," added, "Eventually I made a Kierkegaard collection," which enabled me to "go / Up and down with [Kierkegaard] in his books."[16]

Søren Kierkegaard (1813–1855) is the godfather of twentieth-century existentialism. Indeed, it has been said that the history of twentieth-century theological and philosophical thought flows from conflicting readings of his enigmatic writings.

Kierkegaard took his stand in opposition to the philosophy of G. W. F. Hegel (1770–1831), who deploys a dialectic of thesis, antithesis, and synthesis to reconcile religion and culture, church and state, good and evil, God and humankind. This dialectic makes God a concept among other concepts in a system that can be debated in classrooms and spelled out in textbooks.

For Kierkegaard, God is not an object of thought, but a Mystery that holds us because we cannot get hold of it.

Just as Kierkegaard insists that God is not an object of thought, so Paul Tillich, whom Thomas singled out as his favorite theologian, resists the way that so much theologizing makes God *a* being, albeit a supernatural one, among other beings; an object whose reality or unreality can be debated. Tillich (1886–1965) maintains that a "God about whose existence or non-existence you can argue is a thing beside others within the universe of existing things." The Divine Being, for Tillich, is "the dimension of depth" in life, the Ground of Being—"that which is ultimate, infinite, unconditional" in our "spiritual life."[17]

Tillich's understanding of God as the Ground of Being rhymes with Thomas's affirmation that God is simply *here*—an unseen *presence* in, with, and under "the unhaloed presences"[18]

16. Thomas, *Collected Poems 1945–1990*, 183; "A Grave Unvisited" ("There are places where I have not been").

17. Tillich, *Theology of Culture*, 5, 7.

18. Thomas, *Collected Poems 1945–1990*, 283; "Suddenly" ("As I had always known").

that surround us in our daily lives. Likewise, Tillich's analysis of "Western industrial society" chimes with Thomas's use of the Machine as a symbol for the age in which we live, an age of science and technology.

Tillich understands "Western industrial society" as a system that destroys "individual freedom, personal decision, and organic community; an analytic rationalism which saps the vital forces of life and transforms everything, including man himself, into an object of calculation and control; a secularized humanism which cuts man and the world off from the creative Source and the ultimate mystery of existence."[19]

Thomas translated Tillich's prose into poetry: "'The body is mine and the soul is mine' / says the machine."[20] While Tillich tells us that "Western industrial society" transforms men and women into objects "of calculation and control," Thomas creates an unforgettable image of production lines programming our habits of consumption:

> The tins marched to the music
> Of the conveyor belt. A billion
> Mouths opened. . . .[21]

THREE LOOSE GROUPINGS

People who identify God in an age of science and technology fall into three loose groupings. On one side are unquestioning believers: They identify God as the supernatural Being who literally speaks to them in the words of their holy books. On the other side are unquestioning unbelievers: They identify God as the fantasy of those who close their eyes to life's miseries and their minds to science's discoveries. In the middle are doubting-believers: They

19. Tillich, *Theology of Culture*, 105–6.

20. Thomas, *Collected Later Poems 1988–2000*, 115; "The body is mine and the soul is mine."

21. Thomas, *Collected Poems 1945–1990*, 225; "Postscript" ("As life improved, their poems").

identify God as the Mystery beckoning them to launch themselves across fathoms of doubt and uncertainty.

Unquestioning believers close their minds to scientific discoveries and other areas of research that question and often reject the historicity of the creation stories and some of the historical narratives found in their scriptures. They continue, however, to use their intelligence to develop and employ technologies that are founded on the scientific theories they reject. They may even justify their fascination with machines by saying that technological devices enable them to fulfill the biblical command to "subdue" the earth.[22]

Just as holy-book literalists close their minds to portions of scientific truth, so do persons who insist there is no God close their hearts to segments of intuitive truth. Many of them, probably most, are open to the passions of human love. And numbers of them respond to the intuited truths of art, literature, and music. But they believe that intuitions of God are the pipe dreams of persons who have not outgrown the Santa Claus stage of life. Also they believe they can adduce evidence proving that God does not exist.

Between those two loose groupings are men and women who take an existentialist approach to identifying God. They absorb the intellect's discoveries that produce doubts about God, and they give full credence to the intuitive faculty's belief in God. Among them is R. S. Thomas.

Thomas took an interest in science, knew the work of Darwin, Einstein, and Heisenberg, understood their theories of evolution, relativity, and indeterminacy, and used their concepts as metaphors in his poems. He also knew the limitations of science, in particular its inability to prove or disprove the existence of God.

Any god that science can deal with is one more *thing* in a universe of things; in fact, an idol, a product engineered and manufactured by the human intellect—a godling marching "to the music / Of the conveyor belt." *I Will Be What I Will Be* transcends the world of things; is beyond the reach of the human mind. A God

22. Gen 1:28.

worthy of our belief, our trust, our faith, is a God who dwells in a darkness that science's brightest light cannot illuminate.

Because Thomas recognized science's limitations, he understood that to identify God in an age of science is to launch one's self on a sea of uncertainty, praying that God, "the bridge builder," will lay down "a causeway."[23] And, occasionally, suddenly, the Mystery at the core of the universe does provide solid footing for the doubting-believer's hesitant walk across fathoms of doubt.

ASCRIBING IDENTITY TO GOD IN AN AGE OF SCIENCE AND TECHNOLOGY

The time has come for summarizing Thomas's work in his "laboratory of the spirit"[24]—his approach to identifying God in an age of science and technology.

God is the *Ground of Being*. For Thomas, God is not a being, not even the highest being, in a world of beings. God transcends the material universe. God eludes human reasoning, no matter how sophisticated, how subtle, the arguments may be. God is the Mystery *beyond* everything that falls within the purview of human intelligence. God is the dimension of depth, the grounding, of all that is. In God, we live and move and have our being. God is our *ambiance.*

To say that God is our *ambiance* is to say that God is *ubiquitous.* But there is something mysterious about this ubiquity. It is *elusive*: Sometimes the *everywhere* God is experienced as *here*; sometimes the *everywhere* God is experienced as *not here.*

This divine elusiveness is captured in a drawing of the Supper at Emmaus attributed to Rembrandt.[25] In tones of brown ink on white paper, heightened with chalk, the artist depicts the moment when the eyes of two disciples "were opened, and they recognized

23. Thomas, *Collected Later Poems 1988–2000*, 311; "Space Walking" ("You, the bridge builder").

24. Thomas, *Collected Poems 1945–1990*, 263; "Emerging" ("Not as in the old days I pray").

25. DeWitt, *Rembrandt and the Face of Jesus*, 24.

[Jesus]; and he vanished from their sight."[26] In the drawing, the disciples, one seated, one standing, have just realized that the stranger who joined them on the Emmaus road is the one whose death they have been mourning.

During their mournful stroll, they lament the fact that Jesus is no longer present in their lives. He has been executed, buried: He is absent. There is an emptiness where he was a fullness. Then, suddenly, someone begins to walk with them, talk with them, interpret the Bible for them. Intrigued, the disciples invite the stranger to join them for supper. He accepts, sits down at the table, takes bread and blesses it. Then, suddenly, as they share the bread, they realize that the stranger is Jesus. He is present. And then, equally suddenly, Jesus is absent.

The elusiveness of that experience of the Risen Jesus is what is captured in the drawing attributed to Rembrandt. Before the two disciples can fully take in the new way they are seeing the man on the other side of the table, the chair in which he has been sitting is, suddenly, empty. Not empty, however, simply as a section of the paper on which nothing is inked in. Rather, the artist has left a hint of clothing on the chair and a suggestion of a presence that has almost but not quite vanished.

What dominates, however, is the artist's presentation of the Risen Jesus as a starburst of light—a nondestructive nuclear explosion in a small room:

> What word so explosive
> as that one Palestinian
> word with the endlessness of its fall-out?[27]

Like fall-out, God is always with us. Like fall-out, God is not always perceived. Like fall-out, God's activity is not contingent upon our perception of it.

To summarize: In an age of science and technology, Thomas identifies God as Ground of Being and Elusive Ubiquity.

---

26. Luke 24:31

27. Thomas, *Collected Poems* 1945–1990, 317; "Nuclear" ("It is not that he can't speak").

The Artist-Scientist God

Thomas sees God as a hyphenation of what we mean by an artist and a scientist:

> I praise you because
> you are artist and scientist
> in one. When I am somewhat
> fearful of your power,
> your ability to work miracles
> with a set-square, I hear
> you murmuring to yourself
> in a notation Beethoven
> dreamed of but never achieved.
> You run off your scales of
> rain water and sea water, play
> the chords of the morning
> and evening light, sculpture
> with shadow, join together leaf
> by leaf, when spring
> comes, the stanzas of
> an immense poem. You speak
> all languages and none,
> answering our most complex
> prayers with the simplicity
> of a flower, confronting
> us, when we would domesticate you
> to our uses, with the rioting
> viruses under our lens.[28]

Thomas could use *scientist* as a metaphor for the Ground of Being, because the structure of the universe, the nature of creation, lends itself to the precise analysis of biologists, chemists, and physicists. The world is responsive, opens itself, to the probing human mind. The heart, however, finds dissection diagrams, chemical formulas, and algebraic equations less than warming. There is an abstractness, a coldness, about scientific calculations. Therefore Thomas uses *artist* as well as scientist as a metaphor for God.

---

28. Ibid., 318; "Praise" ("I praise you because").

God is a composer and performer of music, a sculptor, a poet, a linguist. God answers our prayers by opening our eyes to "the lilies of the field, how they grow."[29] But just when we imagine that we are on the verge of comprehending the Elusive Ubiquity, of grasping the One who is a dynamic combination of Beethoven and Darwin, *I Am Who I Am* confounds our thinking—baffles both the reasons of our mind and the reasons of our heart. Just when we suppose that we know enough about God to domesticate her "to our uses," *I Will Be What I Will Be* confronts us "with the rioting / viruses under our lens."

God is the presence who puzzles our mind but warms our heart.

29. Matt 6:28.

7

"The Best Things in the Bible Are Poetry"

AN OBSERVATION MADE BY R. S. Thomas during my interview with him at the Bull Bay Hotel captures the essence of his theological position: "I can't think of a more striking symbol in life than the cross."

Thomas slipped that assertion into our discussion of the poetic, the metaphoric, nature of Scripture, during which he noted that "it is popular to suppose there is more substance in the other world religions than in Christianity. But it isn't so, is it?" Without pausing, he went on to allude to the popularity of Eastern religions with pop stars, artists, and poets, and said, "The cross is more profound than anything in Buddhism or Taoism. I can't think of a more striking symbol in life than the cross."

By the cross, Thomas means a cross without a carved representation of the body of Jesus—a cross without a tenant. In one poem, he refers to "The tall Cross, / Sombre, untenanted"; in another, he describes himself as a person "nailing his questions / One by one to an untenanted cross."[1]

Thomas's preparation for the priesthood was in the high church Anglican tradition, which does not reject tenanted crosses—crucifixes. Nevertheless, he preferred the cross without a sculpted figure of the dead, or dying, Jesus.

1. Thomas, *Collected Poems* 1945–1990, 159 and 180; "Pietà" ("Always the same hills") and "In Church" ("Often I try").

A Masterwork of Doubting-Belief

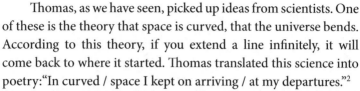

Thomas, as we have seen, picked up ideas from scientists. One of these is the theory that space is curved, that the universe bends. According to this theory, if you extend a line infinitely, it will come back to where it started. Thomas translated this science into poetry:"In curved / space I kept on arriving / at my departures."[2]

Developing that image, he articulated a theology of the cross, in which he combines science's bending universe, the horizontal arms of an everyday signpost, and the Bible's cross of Calvary.

Thomas, as I imagine the scene, stopped his car at a directional sign at a crossroads—a post with two fingerboards, one pointing to a destination to the right, the other to a destination to the left. If, he thought, remembering his reading in modern science, I were to travel infinitely in either direction, I would return, space being curved, to this signpost.

At that moment, this poem began to take shape in his mind:

> . . .
>
> some of us turn aside
>
> to erect the Calvary
> that is our signpost, arms
>
> pointing in opposite directions
> to bring us in the end
>
> to the same place, so impossible
> is it to escape love.[3]

Thomas sees the horizontal crosspiece of the cross of Jesus as a line that can be extended infinitely either to the right or to the left until, in a universe that bends, it comes back to the original intersection—to the place occupied by the crucified Jesus. In the course of that extending and bending, the line inscribes an immense circle in the universe. This circle became a symbol for Thomas of the enveloping love of God. God's infinitely long arms will not let us go—"so impossible / is it to escape love."

2. Ibid., 379; "Pluperfect" ("It was because there was nothing to do").

3. Thomas, *Collected Later Poems* 1988–2000, 195; "The Word" ("Enough that we are on our way").

"I can't think," he said, "of a more striking symbol in life than the cross."

THE BEST THINGS IN THE BIBLE ARE POETRY

Thomas's description of the signpost cross—the "Cross with its arms out pointing both ways"[4]—came at the climax of his response to my question about how he reconciled his two professions: priest and poet. "I am a Bible believer," he said. "I go along with the overall message of the Bible, the best things in which are poetry. There is a strong emphasis in the Bible on metaphor, and a metaphor is a shortcut."

Metaphor uses something we know to give us a hint about something we don't know; something that, most likely, can never be fully known—for example, *I Am Who I Am*. For Christians, Jesus is the supreme metaphor for God. But there are many other God metaphors: rock and spring, king and shepherd, hawk and dove.

"The Bible," Thomas continued, "poses questions that stick in one's mind." As an example, he quoted Jesus's words to his disciples during their last meal together: "This is my body."[5] "How," Thomas wondered, "can this man give me his body to eat? One needs an understanding of metaphor in order to respond."

Then Thomas quoted Jesus's comment about "the sign of Jonah": "An evil and adulterous generation asks for a sign, but no sign shall be given to it except the sign of Jonah."[6] Thomas did not say why he tossed that quote into our conversation. So I was left, as Jesus left his disciples, with the assignment of working out an interpretation.

Thomas's reference to "the sign of Jonah" followed on the heels of his point that the Bible is poetry; that it is essentially metaphoric; that it says one thing *in terms of* something else. The story of Jonah is fiction, not history: An actual Jonah was not swallowed

4. Ibid., 138; "Benedictus" ("Blessed be the starved womb").

5. Matt 26:26; Mark 14:22; Luke 22:19.

6. Matt 16:4.

by an actual whale, no more than an actual Captain Ahab was obsessed with an actual Moby-Dick. The biblical tale of Jonah, like Melville's *Moby-Dick*, like every great novel, is a story that never happened, yet always is true. Always there are people like Jonah trying to escape from God's assignments; always, again like Jonah, there are people trying to flee from the implications of God's love and forgiveness. So while the tale of Jonah is not factual, it is true. People go on trying to escape from God, and God's arms continue to stretch farther than the escapees can run.

The metaphor that is the book of Jonah assures us that God outruns the fastest runner. God is, in Francis Thompson's phrase, "the hound of heaven." God's love is inescapable. That theological insight and others we have been contemplating come together in a poem Thomas published the year I first met him, 1992:

> We have had names for you:
> The Thunderer, the Almighty
> Hunter, Lord of the snowflake
> and the sabre-toothed tiger.
> One name we have held back
> unable to reconcile it
> with the mosquito, the tidal-wave,
> the black hole into which
> time will fall. You have answered
> us with the image of yourself
> on the hewn tree, suffering
> injustice, pardoning it;
> pointing as though in either
> direction; horrifying us
> with the possibility of dislocation.
> Ah, love, with your arms out
> wide, tell us how much more
> they must still be stretched
> to embrace a universe drawing
> away from us at the speed of light.[7]

7. Thomas, *Collected Later Poems* 1988–2000, 170; "Tell Us" ("We have had names for you").

In "Tell Us," the Bible and science are held in a poetic suspension. Thomas begins by listing three names for God that accord well with the nature of supernatural Power that we can read off of nature itself. One name, however, sticks like a fishbone in the human craw.

Love.

We find it hard to square a loving God "with the mosquito, the tidal-wave, / the black hole into which / time will fall." That hole and "a universe drawing / away from us at the speed of light" plant modern science in the poem. Then, with the reference to God's image "on the hewn tree," the Bible enters.

Thomas's God is the suffering, pardoning God, who is edged out of the world onto a cross. Thomas sees the cross as a signpost "pointing as though in either / direction." Then he places the word "dislocation" at the end of a full-stopped line. We bump into a wall. The poem's form on the page, then, imitates the experience of banging our head and becoming disoriented.

Perhaps Thomas wants us to stop dead and think about the *dis-locating* activities of the cross. The cross pulls us out of our customary way of living and thinking, like a hip being pulled out of its socket. The cross dislocates us, then relocates us. It pulls us in two directions, stretching us, so that we can embrace a larger understanding of God and of God's love.

"I Was Trained to Be a Priest; I Wanted to Be a Poet"

Prompted by the fact that poet-priests figure prominently in the literary history of Wales, I asked Thomas: "Has the Welsh tradition of the poet-priest influenced you? In some sense, was your call to ordination a call to be a poet-priest?" Without hesitation, he replied: "No, I was trained to be a priest; I wanted to write poetry. God calls in all kinds of ways. He casts a wide net and sees what he catches."

Thomas had two *callings*: One he experienced as *training* for the priesthood; the other, as a *desire* to be a poet. There was an element of mystery surrounding each vocation: In one, the mystery is called God; in the other, Euterpe, the muse of lyric poetry.

Thomas described his divine summons by alluding to Jesus's declaration that "the kingdom of heaven is like a net that was thrown into the sea and caught fish of every kind."[8] In Thomas's case, God's net caught a boy whose mother thought he should be a priest, whose father voiced no objection to the idea, and who himself felt a certain priestly inclination.

"Did any priests," I wondered, "influence you as a child and then as an adolescent?" "No," Thomas answered, "I was unfortunate in that respect."

"What was the churchmanship at the church hostel in Bangor?"—a residence hall for budding theologs at the University of North Wales. His response indicated that it was high church: "Confession was available. But I never went. Bells rang at the Sursum Corda. The warden wore vestments. There was incense. But such was not my way. You must believe intensely in high church liturgy to inflict it on the people of rural Wales. It is foreign to them. My churchmanship was moderate—the easy way."

Thomas continued to disclose his "easy way" as he talked about British Nonconformity, which comprises denominations that refuse to conform to the doctrines, liturgies, and disciplines of the Church of England, the church established by law. Principal among these Nonconformists are Presbyterians, Congregationalists, Methodists, Quakers, and Baptists. Although the Church in Wales, a sister of the Church of England, was no longer legally established when Thomas was ordained priest, he still saw it as *the* embodiment of the Christian tradition in Wales.

"There were Christians in Wales," Thomas told me, "when England was still pagan. The Christian tradition of Wales was *catholic*—first, Roman; then, Anglican. Nonconformity was a latecomer to Wales. Its successes in the eighteenth and nineteenth centuries have led to the impression of Wales being a Nonconformist country. Yet it is the Church in Wales that represents the older, more dominant tradition."

8. Matt 13:47.

The Nonconformists saved the Welsh language, Thomas thought. He continued: "I am a Nonconformist at heart. I like the concept of the gathered church, the sense of independence. But the problem with Nonconformity lies in what happens in the practice of Nonconformity. Nonconformist chapels are not aesthetically pleasing. I could not worship God with my whole being in the average Nonconformist chapel. Churches, on the other hand, possess the aura of being earlier, more traditional."

Thomas preferred church buildings in which Welsh Christians had worshiped for centuries. "The smaller, the simpler the church building," he said, "the more it pleases me." To worship rightly, Thomas needed a place of simple beauty, hallowed by tradition, evoking stillness.

The second quarrel he had with Nonconformity was with its understanding of the role of the ordained minister. "I resent," he said, "the displacing of the traditional concept of the priest leading his congregation up into the presence of God. In the rural parishes I've served, the people look up to the priest, see him as the mediator." When celebrating the Eucharist, Thomas stood between the people and the altar, with his back to the congregation, looking across the altar to the chancel window. "I prefer," he said, "to be a traditionalist, to lead the people up to the presence of God; not to stand behind the altar, as if I were standing at a shop counter with something to sell."

"I also object to Nonconformity," he continued, "because in Nonconformity the sacrament of the Word displaces the sacrament of the Elements. Simple, uneducated people should be taught to worship more than to understand. The element of mystery is more important than learned sermons." Thomas added that "the genius of Christianity is the Sacrament—take the bread and wine and make them into symbols"—transform them into metaphors, into poetry. He did not, he insisted, "belittle the Word." Indeed, he went on, "Anglicanism at its best gives equal value to Word and Sacrament, thus dealing with the Roman Catholic heresy of overemphasizing the Sacrament. Nonconformity overemphasizes the Word, thereby reversing the Roman Catholic heresy."

Summarizing Thomas's lowish high-churchmanship: He opted for small, simple places of worship, preferably centuries old, in which the focal point is the altar, not the pulpit. On the altar, an untenanted cross and candles. On the priest, black cassock and white surplice, not the eucharistic vestments that change colors as the seasons of the church year change. Not for Thomas the "smells and bells" of highish churchmanship.

As a traditionalist, Thomas stood apart from the high church worship developed in the nineteenth century and from many aspects of the liturgical revival of the twentieth century. "Modern liturgists," he argued, "make a mistake. They try in the Eucharist to recreate a social meal. They gather the people *around* the table. They want to return to the upper room by putting the priest behind the altar. But you can't regain the intimacy of the Last Supper in the upper room. Therefore I prefer to be a traditionalist, to lead the people up to the presence of God."

"I Am Guilty of the Love of Created Things"

Continuing to talk about his university days, Thomas recalled that "Evelyn Underhill gave a talk on mysticism while I was at Bangor." Underhill (1875–1941) wrote one of the twentieth century's most influential books on mysticism. But, Thomas said, "I played O's and X's with my neighbor in the lecture hall. I was not spiritually or intellectually ready for what Underhill had to say. I have an instinctive hostility to mysticism; I don't take to it at all. I am guilty of the love of created things; devoted to the sacrament of language"—dedicated to the rite of poetry.

Moving on to his theological college days, Thomas remembered: "There were weekly sessions during which you were to sit at your desk and meditate. But I never could meditate—tried, but always started composing a poem. Once a term, there were quiet days, retreats. We were not to speak; we ate in silence; we attended talks on devotion. Some students would meet around the corner after lunch and go for a walk. I did not go for a walk, but I did not necessarily spend my time meditating."

"There was a slight air of unreality" he recalled, "at St. Michael's," his theological college. "The warden read from the writings of St. Francis, about how Francis pushed his fingers into the food of lepers." With a tone of disdain, Thomas termed it "unreality." "George Herbert," he added, "was that sort of person."

The St. Michael's faculty made vague attempts to teach care of the parish, "but what was taught," he continued, "was useless in a country parish. We had Old and New Testament studies at St. Michael's; doctrine to acquaint us with orthodoxy. All of us students treated these subjects as necessary on the way to ordination." Outside the classroom, "students discussed theological subjects, argued about them."

"Theologically, I suppose I was influenced by Dean Inge, F. R. Tennant, and W. R. Matthews, who were put before me at St. Michael's." William Ralph Inge (1860–1954), nicknamed "The Gloomy Dean" of St. Paul's Cathedral in London, was a theologian, the author of more than thirty books, and a columnist for the *Evening Standard* for twenty-five years. He advocated personal faith resting upon experience and individual inspiration, as opposed to faith based on dogmatic authority.

Philosophical theology was the specialty of Frederick Robert Tennant (1866–1957). In particular, he sought to harmonize science and religion, maintaining that the ordering of nature points to a divine Designer. Stressing the aesthetic appeal of nature, he said: "God reveals Himself . . . in many ways; and some men enter His Temple by the Gate Beautiful."[9]

Walter Robert Matthews (1881–1973) followed Inge as Dean of St. Paul's and, like Inge, was a theological journalist, writing for the *Daily Telegraph*. He too, in books such as *God in Christian Experience*, focused on the individual's encounters with God, rather than on dogmatic assertions.

Perhaps Thomas was influenced by a concern shared by Matthews, Tennant, and Inge. They worried that science and religion would agree to a more or less amicable divorce. Thomas thought

9. Tennant, *Philosophical Theology*, 2:93.

that science and religion should live in a tension-filled marriage; each having their say, neither being allowed to outshout the other.

No doubt he also responded positively to the interest that Inge, Tennant, and Matthews took in the individual's personal experience of God, and the way they played down creeds and dogmas. And Tennant's stress on the aesthetic appeal of nature—on entering God's temple by the Gate Beautiful—would have caught the attention of Thomas, who said he was "guilty of the love of created things."

Thomas recognized, however, that the world's "created things" point to a Creator who is not all sweetness and light. Inside the Gate Beautiful lurk things that are benevolent and things that are malevolent. In other words, if the world discloses God, then God is Lord of both snowflake and saber-toothed tiger. So, in Thomas's view, when we are assessing what created things tell us about God, we must pay close attention to *all* created things. Dealing theologically with the world's cherries, while using doctrinal stratagems to hide the pits, is simply disingenuous.

Thomas was like a camera without filters—like an unblinking eye:

> . . . I am eyes
> Merely, witnessing virtue's
> Defeat; seeing the young born
> Fair, knowing the cancer
> Awaits them. One thing I have asked
> Of the disposer of the issues
> Of life: that truth should defer
> To beauty. It was not granted.[10]

Thomas learned to live and believe without having his questions answered, his doubts resolved. Believing was not a sort of alchemy for him; it did not change leaden reality into golden truth. His belief in God did not trump the doubts raised by his observations of the world and of life, nor did the doubts raised by his observations trump his belief in God.

10. Thomas, *Collected Poems* 1945–1990, 209; "Petition" ("And I standing in the shade").

IDENTIFYING ADDITIONAL INFLUENCES

I continued, during my interview with Thomas, to press him about theologians who influenced him. A curiosity question elicited a hint about a contributor, in addition to Inge, Tennant, and Matthews, to his resistance to orthodox metaphysics: "What," I asked, "is the identity of E. E. T. in your poem 'In Memoriam E. E. T.'?" Thomas answered: "He was Edward Evan Thomas, the rector of a neighboring parish when I was a curate, the godfather of my son. He had studied under Harnack."

Adolf Harnack (1851–1930), a professor of church history at Berlin, mastered early Christian literature, becoming his generation's outstanding interpreter of the thinking of the theologians of the first four or five Christian centuries—the philosophically inclined thinkers who turned the teachings of Jesus and the writings of Paul into creeds, dogmas, and systematic theologies. Harnack's widely influential conclusion is that the metaphysics supporting Christian doctrines and dogmas is an intrusion from Greek philosophy into Christian teaching.

Thomas said that he appreciated E. E. Thomas, with whom he had long talks about "Harnack / and the mind's reach."[11] Part of "the mind's reach," no doubt, was Harnack's contention that Greek metaphysics invaded Christian thought in the way that English kings invaded Wales; in each instance something glorious, something true, was lost.

Thomas, no doubt with Harnack in mind, called the doctrine of the Trinity a complication "by Greek thought" of the biblical message "that God is one." Thomas went on to say that "the philosophy of the Trinity with its idea of Three in One and One in Three provided, in the opinion of the sophisticated, a better description of the mystery of God."[12] Thomas, however, questioned whether sophisticated Greek philosophy is the best way to present the mysterious *I Am Who I Am*.

---

11. Ibid., 454; "In Memoriam E. E. T." ("Young I offered an old man").

12. Anstey, *Thomas: Selected Prose*, 143, 144.

Thomas also thought that Paul initiated the process of complicating Christianity. In Thomas's words, Paul is "the mountain / the teaching of the carpenter of Nazareth / congealed into." Thomas sees Paul as the one who began turning the life and teachings of Jesus into rock-hard theological systems. This leaves us "staring / across deep crevices at conclusions at which / the living Jesus would not willingly have arrived."[13]

Thomas's long talks with E. E. Thomas about Harnack may well underlie this assertion: "An admirer of the Middle / Ages, I disengage from their dogma."[14] In another poem, Thomas sees the God described by theologians in their learned tomes "as an idea, / crumbled by their dry / minds in the long sentences / of their chapters, gathering dust / in their libraries; . . ."[15]

As my interview with Thomas moved on, I asked if Martin Luther's "theology of the cross" influenced him. "I have never read any Luther, any Barth. I'm rather thin in theology. I know nothing about patristics. Meister Eckhart, however, was an eye-opener. He was closer to twentieth-century views than more orthodox theologians."

Eckhart did all he could to steer Christians away from the idea that they understood God; that their way of expressing the meaning of God was the complete and perfect way of articulating God's nature and ways. That type of dogmatic self-confidence was, Eckhart thought, the greatest of theological errors.

Thomas translates Eckhart's insight into poetry, writing that God's "resistance / is endless at the frontier of the great poem."[16] God resists our attempts to lock up God in "the great poem" of our theological statements—statements that make it impossible

---

13. Thomas, *Collected Poems* 1945–1990, 406; "Covenanters" ("He wore no hat, but he produced, say").

14. Thomas, *Collected Later Poems* 1988–2000, 351; "Temptation" ("Not a door between us, nor a gate").

15. Ibid., 150; "The God" ("Made of rhyme and metre").

16. Thomas, *Collected Poems* 1945–1990, 291; "The Combat" ("You have no name").

for God to catch her breath. Thomas imagines God laboring to breathe "within the confines / of our definition of him."[17]

Thomas's Approach to Theological Thinking

Three things need to be said about Thomas's approach to theological thinking. They echo, with Thomas's distinctive nuances, some of the theologians whose works he read.

First, he held Bible belief and science together, identifying their points of contact; refusing, however, to force them into false harmony. Thomas gave full weight to what the Bible tells us about God, always remembering that biblical language is essentially metaphoric, poetic. He also gave full weight to what science tells us about the world, its origin and evolution. Always, however, he remembered that from their earliest days human beings have intuited truths from a realm that the scientific mind cannot penetrate.

The first part, then, of Thomas's approach to theological thinking is one of holding belief in God and the truths of science in creative tension, encouraging each to speak its piece, allowing neither to outshout the other.

Secondly, Thomas assigned more importance to experiences of God's presence and absence than to dogmatic formulas and systematic theologies. As his interpretation of the cross makes clear, he did not ignore the central beliefs of the Christian faith. But he was far from supposing that declaring allegiance to a list of fundamental beliefs defines a relationship with God. To have such a relationship means waiting in hungering silence to experience the presence or absence of the elusive God.

Finally, Thomas hyphenated his priestly calling and his bardic calling, thereby becoming a poet-theologian. This set him apart from the prose theologians who have dominated theology for nearly two thousand years.

Thomas's poems mirror the bazaar of God-ideas found in the Bible. Except for the book of Esther, in which God is not

17. Ibid., 358; "The White Tiger" ("It was beautiful as God").

mentioned, the Bible overflows with God talking to humans and humans talking about God—God's talk and God-talk. Prose theologians boil down all this talk to produce a theological syrup that is so gummy that God gets stuck in it. In the process, the Bible's theological smorgasbord is lost.

The Bible offers diverse, often contradictory, theological insights that make the point that God is fundamentally *unknowable*.

God may be experienced, but not known. There is, to use the title of a fourteenth-century classic of Christian literature, *a cloud of unknowing* between us and God. As a poet-theologian, Thomas preserves that cloud. His poems reflect the Bible's God-talk and God's talk, both of which in their variety serve to keep us from supposing that we understand God, that we *know* God.

Thomas, following the lead of the biblical authors, gives us poems in which he tells us about his experiences of the elusive God and poems in which the speaker is God. And while prose theologians develop doctrines of free will and original sin, Thomas, imitating the Bible, tells us stories about men and women, what they do and how they think. The Bible shows us David watching Bathsheba bathe. Thomas shows us Davies, a chapel deacon, watching a girl during a worship service:

> Are your heart's coals
> Kindled for God, or is the burning
> Of your lean cheeks because you sit
> Too near that girl's smouldering gaze?[18]

God's Hyphen

God's hyphen, the cross's horizontal piece of timber, made it possible for Thomas to hyphenate the Bible and science, his experiences of God and his thinking about God, his priestly and his bardic callings, and his doubt and his belief.

As we have seen, when the two ends of the crosspiece are extended infinitely in curved space, they return to where they started,

18. Ibid., 76; "Chapel Deacon" ("Who put that crease in your soul").

thereby inscribing a circle in the universe, which is a metaphor, in Thomas's theology, for the encircling arms of God.

God's hyphen, then, holds together realities that strain to pull farther and farther apart. It ties together science and the Bible, English and Welsh, poet and priest, *boulevardier* and moor-walker, believer and unbeliever. As Paul told the Galatians, "There is no longer Jew or Greek, there is no longer slave or free, there is no longer male and female; for all of you are one in Christ Jesus."[19]

19. Gal 3:28.

8

"My Health Seems to Have Completely Broken Down"

I WASN'T THINKING ABOUT a time when I'd remember last good-byes as I helped Betty Vernon wrap up in a soft woolen shawl and watched Ronald Thomas collect her at the door of the Bull Bay Hotel on November 11, 1994, Remembrance Day in Britain.

In the event, however, that is my memory of our last good-bye. Letters passed back and forth over the next six years, but we never met again. And then, when Thomas's last letter arrived in early April 2000, I did not know it was his last, although he said: "My health seems to have completely broken down through heart trouble."

Previous letters had announced that he was no longer able to do this or that, only to be followed by a letter mentioning a visit to Spain or Oman or Egypt. So wouldn't the mail carrier bring another light blue aerogramme with Thomas's distinctive hand-writing? No. His "With kind thoughts, Ronald" of March 31, 2000, was his last sign-off.

NOMINEE FOR THE NOBEL PRIZE FOR LITERATURE

Some ten days after Nancy and I said goodbye to Ronald and Betty at the Bull Bay Hotel, we were back in the States. Thanksgiving morning, I finished transcribing the notes of my interview with

Thomas, and sent him a thank you letter. Three days earlier, Betty had written to Nancy:

> Cefn Du Ganol, Llanfairynghornwy, Anglesey
> November 20, 1994
>
> Dear Mrs. McEllhenney—
>
> Thank you so much for asking us to supper—it is always fun to have a meal "out" and I think that the hotel you stayed in has a lovely "facing the sea" view.
>
> I expect that you are now back and very busy getting ready for Christmas—at least you could shop in the various places you stayed and your family will enjoy their surprise presents.
>
> All the very best wishes for Christmas and 1995
> Betty Vernon

Sometime in December, I looked for a Christmas gift that would tell Thomas about the area where I lived, Pennsylvania's Chester County. Often I drove along the Brandywine River, passing Andrew Wyeth's home, to reach the Brandywine River Museum. So when, while browsing in the museum shop, my eye chanced upon *The Brandywine* by Henry Seidel Canby, with illustrations by Wyeth, I bought it for Thomas.

> Cefn Du Ganol, Llanfairynghornwy,
> Holyhead, Gwynedd LL65 4LG
> January 6, 1995
>
> Dear John
>
> Thank you very much for the gift of *The Brandywine*. I hope I get time to read it before long.
>
> I trust you had a pleasant Christmas and have now settled down to work again. I'm afraid I will not be available when you bring your party over this summer. I am retiring from readings and public engagements from this year on. I have been around too long really and in any

case travelling around takes it out of me even when I am not driving.

Good wishes to you both in '95
Ronald

When I next wrote to Thomas, I enclosed a copy of a letter from the editor who was considering my book proposal:

> One thing I do not doubt is that we would have a fine product in the book itself. My brief exposure to the Thomas poetry through your material indicates that he is everything you say he is, and that he deserves a much wider audience. Poetry, as you know, comes and goes in popularity—although I don't know how long the cycles last. I had hopes when I attended the Clinton inauguration and heard Maya Angelou, but while there has certainly been a renewal of interest in her own work, that renewal has not extended to poetry in general. Such missed opportunities make it hard to sell poetry!

I remembered Thomas's March 29 birthday, and wrote to him again in July. Among other things, I said that Nancy and I had heard that he had "been nominated for the Nobel Prize for Literature. Our most hearty congratulations! We shall be looking forward with eager anticipation to the announcement in November. Of course, I shall use your nomination to see if I can hurry the publisher's response to my book proposal."

I heard about Thomas's Nobel nomination from an English friend, who sent this article from the *Independent on Sunday*:

> R S Thomas, the cantankerous clergyman who is Wale's most important living poet, is being nominated for the Nobel Prize for Literature by powerful figures in the British literary establishment. . . .

> Thomas's [nomination] will be made by the Welsh Academy with the support of last year's winner, Kenzaburo Oe, who was bowled over by Thomas's writing. . . .

He refused initially to agree to be nominated before yielding grudgingly on condition that if he won he could make his acceptance speech in his beloved Welsh. . . .

"I don't know anything about the mechanics of the business, but one can only be grateful if anybody thinks you are worth putting up," [Thomas] said. "It's sort of local boy made good and I imagine that all over the world there are minorities putting up their champions."[1]

Several months passed, then Thomas, having driven by the hotel where Nancy and I had dinner with him and Betty the previous November, wrote:

Llanfairynghornwy, Holyhead, LL65 4LG, Cymru (Wales)
October 6, 1995

Dear John

Thank you for your letters. I was passing the hotel near Amlwch this afternoon and thought it was time I answered them.

I seem to have been busy doing nothing the last few months, and will be even more busy for the next two. There is a conference of minority cultures in Barcelona in November, where I will be part of the Welsh delegation. Then in December there is a 5-capital reading tour of the British Isles for the Arts Council.

My nomination for the Nobel award is for next year, but as Heaney has had it for 1995 they are unlikely to give it to a poet again next year—not this poet anyway. This has all been about me. I hope you and Nancy are well and happy and doing interesting things.

Yours sincerely
Ronald

---

1. Marianne Macdonald, "R S Thomas nominated for Nobel Prize," *Independent on Sunday*, July 9, 1995.

A Masterwork of Doubting-Belief

"Reading R. S. Thomas" in Japan

Thomas's nomination for the 1996 Nobel Prize was endorsed, as we have seen, by Kenzaburo Oe, recipient of the prize in 1994. Oe, "who was bowled over by Thomas's writing," had been pondering Thomas's poems in Tokyo, with the result that "Reading R. S. Thomas" is the title of one chapter in Oe's novel *Somersault*. Oe uses Thomas's poems to move his story forward, but what interests us is his choice of poems—ones that feature themes we have been considering: the silence of God, the leap of faith, "the absence/ of clamour" when God comes, Kierkegaard's "walk over seventy thousand fathoms," and wearing "your eyes out" watching for a rare bird's coming.[2] One of Oe's characters quotes several sentences from Kierkegaard's *Concluding Unscientific Postscript* to make a point that we have dealt with in Thomas's poems:

> Without risk there is no faith. Faith is precisely the contradiction between the infinite passion of the individual's inwardness and the objective uncertainty. If I am capable of grasping God objectively, I do not believe, but precisely because I cannot do this I must believe.[3]

Two Prizes, But Not the Nobel

Following my custom, I looked for a Chester County gift to send to Thomas at Christmas 1995. What I found was a print of a portrait by Andrew Wyeth of his wife. Because of Wyeth's photo-like style, Thomas, responding in early January, refers to it as a "photograph":

2. Thomas, *Collected Poems* 1945–1990, 283, 362, 306; "Suddenly" ("As I had always known"), "Balance" ("No piracy, but there is a plank"), and "Seawatching" ("Grey waters, vast").

3. Oe, *Somersault*, 76.

Llanfairynghornwy, Holyhead, LL65 4LG
January 22, 1996

Dear John

I have left answering your Christmas messages rather late, but I have been thinking about you in the problems that your massive snowfall must have caused. We have had nothing comparable, but then this is a mild area. I believe it was bad in Scotland before Christmas.

Thank you very much for the photograph of Wyeth's wife.

We wish you both good things this year.

Yours sincerely
Ronald

I wrote again in September, spoke about my eager anticipation of the announcement of the Nobel Prize, enclosed a copy of my recently published short biography of John Wesley, and told him that work on the townhouse Nancy and I were buying for our retirement home was nearing completion. Thomas replied:

Llanfairynghornwy, Holyhead, LL65 4LG, Môn, Cymru
October 8, 1996

Dear John

I'm not sure whether I owe you thanks for other letters apart from your last with its pamphlet enclosed.

I have been visiting about a bit, and also spent 10 days in Scotland on the Isle of Islay.

I was lucky enough to be awarded a Lannan prize recently, which will boost my finances a bit. Fortunately one is not expected to travel to Los Angeles to receive it! I refused to go to Ohio recently, although I have to go to Munich in December to receive a prize there. I hope the building proceeds before the snow comes.

Yours sincerely
Ronald

The 1996 Nobel Prize recipient was announced either shortly before or immediately after Thomas wrote, but at no time did he say anything to me about the recipient, the Polish poet Wisława Szymborska. As Thomas's letter indicates, he did receive two literary prizes in 1996, the Lannan Lifetime Achievement Award for Poetry, which boosted his finances by $50,000, and the Horst Bienek Prize for Poetry from the Bavarian Academy of Fine Arts. The citation for the Lannan Award notes that Thomas called literature "the communication of thought and emotion at the highest and most articulate level. It is the supreme human statement."

SECOND MARRIAGE

With my 1996 Christmas greeting, I enclosed a book about the Christmas tree ornaments created from natural materials by volunteers at the Brandywine River Museum, and said:

> Dear Betty and Ronald:
>
> According to the London *Observer* of 10 November, you married recently. Nancy and I send you our affectionate best wishes.
>
> May this Christmas season be a blessed one and the year 1997 a good and healthy one.
>
> Best wishes,
> John

Thomas replied on New Year's Day:

> Cefn Du Ganol, Llanfairynghornwy,
> Holyhead, Gwynedd, LL65 4LG
> January 1, 1997
>
> Dear John
>
> Thank you very much for your Christmas message and the book.

We travelled a bit at the end of the year, to the U.A.E. and Oman to watch birds, and then to Munich to receive a prize from the Bavarian Academy of Fine Arts, thanks to the versions of my poems which Kevin Perryman has made.

Betty and I married in August, but now her daughter is very ill and we have to go over to-morrow to be around.

With our best wishes to you both for this new year
Ronald

There's a matter-of-factness in Thomas's reference to Betty's daughter's illness. Certainly, conventional expressions of emotional warmth and love were not part of his nature, and he himself, in a 1999 interview, said: "I don't think I'm a very loving person. I wasn't brought up in a loving home—my mother was afraid of emotion—and you tend to carry on in the same way don't you? I'm always ready to confess the things that are lacking in me and particularly this lack of love for human beings."[4]

It's important, I think, to accept Thomas's confession, but not to use it to present him as an austere, uncaring man—as a face of stone. Indeed, this chapter's letters reveal that he cared about others, but in his own way, which was lacking in gush.

Following my greeting to Thomas on his eighty-fourth birthday, he sent a postcard:

Many thanks for remembering my birthday. I hope yours will be a happy day, too.

Best wishes
Ronald

My next letter, written on the Fourth of July, noted that I had retired from the pastorate. Also I said that Nancy and I were considering another trip to Wales in 1998. Several weeks later, Thomas wrote:

4. Brown, *R. S. Thomas*, 98.

Llanfairynghornwy, Holyhead LL65 4LG
July 30, 1997

Dear John

Thank you for your last letter. I have already lost your new address, so I hope the old one reaches you.

I am glad you had a good retirement party and have found a good place to retire to.

I am getting pretty decrepit now, so don't feel like making any plans to meet in the future.

Betty's only daughter died aged 40 in March, so that was a cruel blow, making us ask why geriatrics like us should be spared.

With best wishes
Ronald

Responding to the news of the death of Betty's daughter, I wrote Betty a sympathy letter, to which Thomas replied:

Llanfairynghornwy
[no date, indistinct postmark]
[received fall 1997]

Dear John

It was good of you to send such a kind letter and Betty much appreciated it. She misses Alice terribly—to think she wasn't even half our age, and we are spared.

I hope you are enjoying your new home.

We were in Dublin the other day and met Czeslaw Milosz, the Polish poet, who is actually a Lithuanian. As far as I can tell from translation, he is a major poet.

All is relatively quiet on this home front.

With all good wishes,
Ronald

I sent a Christmas 1997 greeting, but kept no record of it. Just after Christmas, Thomas wrote:

> Llanfairynghornwy
> December 29, 1997
>
> Dear John
>
> Thank you for your Christmas wishes. I have a feeling there was another letter I should have answered. Please forgive me.
>
> We went to the Middle East in November and became tourists, gawping at the pyramids, Luxor and Petra etc. Betty still has an appetite for travel.
>
> There has been a lot of dissatisfaction of late because of a hurricane on Christmas Eve—telephone and electric cables down. A poor Christmas for some.
>
> Anyway have a good year both of you.
> Ronald

Beginning in 1998, it is difficult for me to tell what I said to Thomas. Having retired, I had time to write longhand letters, of which I made no copies. Judging from his response, I sent a book of Monet reproductions for his eighty-fifth birthday:

> Llanfairynghornwy, Holyhead, Ynys Môn, LL65 4LG
> [no date, indistinct postmark]
> [probably early April 1998]
>
> Dear John
>
> It was kind of you to remember my birthday and to send such a pleasant book on Monet. As you know, I love the Impressionists. We spent the week end in Dublin, where Betty went shopping. She still grieves for Alice.
>
> We are moving house at the end of April. I will send you the address and telephone number later. It is a smaller cottage near Porthmadog.
>
> With best wishes to you both
> Ronald

My next letter, written in early July, reports:

> At long last, the editor of *Quarterly Review* has accepted
> an article I wrote about your poetry. It will run in 1999,
> probably the summer issue. *QR* is the scholarly journal
> for United Methodist clergy.
>
> May 1 was not a happy day for us. As we were driving
> home from a Philadelphia Orchestra concert, a driver
> headed down hill toward us hit his brakes on a rain-slick
> road, slid, and plowed into the left front of our car. Nancy
> suffered a fractured rib and nasty bruises. My bruises
> healed more quickly. The car was a total loss.

Thomas responded almost immediately:

> Tŷ Main, Llanfrothen, Gwynedd, LL48 6SG
> July 23, 1998
>
> Dear John
>
> Thank you for your letter, though I was sorry to hear
> about your accident. I hope Nancy's rib has mended. I'm
> glad you are getting somewhere with your article on my
> work.
>
> After many delays we are in our cottage, still trying to
> impose order. I have lost sight of the sea although it is
> only some 3 or 4 miles away. This is the pick of Welsh
> mountain scenery. I can see Snowdon from just outside
> the cottage and other mountains are about us, though
> they do not pass the qualifying altitude of 3000 feet.
>
> With best wishes
> Ronald

There were no further letters from Thomas in 1998, and I
have no idea what form my Christmas greeting took. But again he
responded on New Year's Day:

Llanfrothen, Gwynedd, LL48 6SG
January 1, 1999

Dear John

Thank you for your letter, card and greetings, which reached us in good time.

This is to wish you both success in the New Year.

I am trying to acquire copies of 'An Acre of Land' and 'The Minister' but not having much success, so if you come across them, please buy them, and I will re-imburse you gladly.

Well, poetry is the worse for losing Ted Hughes, although I don't think 'Birthday Letters' is his best work. Still, Plath has always caught the imagination of most readers.

I wish you and Nancy a happy and successful year.
Ronald

English Poet Laureate Ted Hughes died on October 28, 1998. Thomas spoke of Hughes as a modern poet he read with appreciation; and Hughes's early books of poetry, in particular *Crow*, may have influenced Thomas's own poetic style. Hughes was married to American poet Sylvia Plath from 1956 until her death in 1963. The year Hughes died, he published *Birthday Letters*—poems addressed to Plath and written over the years after her death.

Although I checked every catalog I received from rare book dealers, and contacted the ones I knew personally, I was unable to locate copies for Thomas of his second and third books. Apparently, I sent Thomas a book for his eighty-sixth birthday.

Tŷ Main , Llanfrothen, Gwynedd
April 15, 1999

Dear John

It was very kind of you to remember my birthday and to send the book, which I am about half-way through. I can't read for long any more without falling asleep! Senility not Alzheimer, I hope.

We have found a copy of 'An Acre of Land' so now need only 'The Minister'.

We shall be moving house of May 5th to Twll y Cae, Pentrefelin, Cricieth, Gwynedd, LL52 OPU – about 6 miles west of here. This cottage is far too small.

With remembrances to you both and felicitations on your coming 40th anniversary.

Ronald

"My World Stock Fluctuates a Good Deal!"

Nancy and I celebrated our fortieth wedding anniversary by visiting a number of America's national parks. Sometime after returning home, I sent him pictures from the Badlands of South Dakota; also in the package was a copy of the Fall 1999 issue of *Quarterly Review* containing my article titled "R. S. Thomas: Poet for Turn-of-Millennium Believers." Early in November, Thomas acknowledged those items:

Twll y Cae, Pentrefelin, Cricieth, Gwynedd
November 3, 1999

Dear John

Thank you very much for your article, which I was interested to read. It is good of you to go to the trouble of trying to interest readers in my work. My world stock fluctuates a good deal! Some unexpected countries like Sweden and Italy seem quite keen, while others like the old colonies, Australia, New Zealand, South Africa etc are apathetic, and the United States, appreciative in the older parts, Louisiana, Texas, Arkansas while disinterested in the trendy New York, Boston area.

I was grateful for your fine photographs. I was familiar with references to the Badlands, but had never actually seen pictures. I'm sure they are bad for people and good for birds! I'm glad you keep your hand in teaching.

With our kind thoughts to you
Ronald

The University of Arkansas Press published *Poems of R. S. Thomas* (1985), a selection of poems from his earlier books; *R. S. Thomas* (1990), a study of the poet and his poetry by W. Moelwyn Merchant; and *Miraculous Simplicity: Essays on R. S. Thomas* (1993). The latter volume is edited by William V. Davis, a major interpreter of Thomas's poetry, who is professor of English and writer-in-residence at Baylor University in Waco, Texas, which Thomas pronounced "Wacko." Thomas's next letter, his last, arrived in early April 2000, thanking me for my gift for his eighty-seventh birthday, a small volume of portrait faces from the National Gallery in London. He observed that in default of the better, that is, not being able to view the original paintings, he enjoyed reproductions.

Twll y Cae, Pentrefelin, Cricieth, Cymru LL52 0PU
No date; postmarked March 31, 2000

Dear John

That was a very nice gift you sent me on my birthday. Thank you. Faute de mieux I enjoy reproductions of great paintings. I have seen very few originals.

I hope you have escaped the snow and winds which seem to have been getting rather out of hand in the States and some other countries. We seem to be in a fairly sheltered pocket here, and being just 2½ miles between Porthmadog and Cricieth, it is very convenient for the few things we need domestically.

My health seems to have completely broken down through heart trouble and I can do little more than drive the car and hobble between shops. The medication

> makes me sleepy, so I can no longer concentrate long enough to write a poem.
>
> I hope you and Nancy are in better shape.
>
> With kind thoughts
> Ronald

Thomas died on September 25, 2000; his ashes are buried in a churchyard at Porthmadog, not far from his last home. A tribute service was held in Westminster Abbey on March 28, 2001, the day before what would have been his eighty-eighth birthday. It was led by Poet Laureate Andrew Motion, who, along with poets Seamus Heaney, Gillian Clarke, and John Burnside, read a selection of Thomas's poems. In the course of this reading, Motion realized something that had not occurred to him before: "I had been aware that some of the poems were similar, and that night I realized why this was. They were all fragments of a Masterwork."[5]

A MASTERWORK OF DOUBTING-BELIEF

Each of Thomas's poems is a segment of a masterwork of doubting-belief. He created a body of work for those of us who, like the father in Mark's Gospel, cry out, "I believe; help my unbelief!"[6]

Thomas's poetry helps our unbelief by indicating that doubting-belief is not flawed faith; not a believer's failure to respond wholeheartedly to the revelation of God. Rather, doubting-belief is the human response that correlates with God's self-revelation. Doubting-belief corresponds to the way God chooses to be concealed and revealed.

God comes to us, suddenly, as the risen Jesus came to the disciples on the road to Emmaus. For a time, we don't realize that what we sense is God's mysterious presence. Then, in the moment of recognition, just as our heart burns within us, God, suddenly, is absent once more. So while experiences of God's presence

---

5. Rogers, *Man Who Went Into the West*, 315.
6. Mark 9:24.

make belief possible, experiences of God's absence make doubt inevitable.

Thomas, then, helps our unbelief by writing poems that show us that doubt flows from a choice made by God—the divine decision to be elusive. Because God chooses to be here one moment, not here the next, we doubt *and* believe.

Finally, Thomas helps our unbelief by expressing his own belief in God—God understood as the Ground of Being, the Great Unifier, the One who makes all things one. In the words of Wordsworth, *I Am Who I Am* is "central peace, subsisting at the heart / Of endless agitation."

Thomas says that "it is to the prophets of Israel that we must look for the first vision of the being who united everyone and everything in and through himself." Then, quoting the Islamic affirmation of faith, he continues: "There is no God but God. This is what exists at the centre of things, the unity in which everyone can see the reason for, and the meaning of, the life of the whole of creation and of their own little personal lives."[7] This vision, as we have seen, becomes flesh for Thomas at Calvary: "I can't think of a more striking symbol in life than the cross."

Thomas visualizes the horizontal bar of the cross as a line that can be extended infinitely until, in a universe that bends, it comes back to the original intersection—to the place occupied by the crucified Jesus. In the course of that extending and bending, the line inscribes an immense circle in the universe. This circle became a symbol for Thomas of the unifying love of God. God's infinitely long arms will not let us go—"so impossible / is it to escape love."

THE LAST WORD

Thomas, in his second letter, urged me to read *Counterpoint*, a book in which belief and doubt make points and counterpoints. His last word, however, is found in two poems on facing pages

7. Anstey, *Thomas: Selected Prose*, 144.

at the book's conclusion—poems of confidence in the God of the infinitely large embrace:

> When we are weak, we are
> strong. When our eyes close
> on the world, then somewhere
> within us the bush
>
> burns. When we are poor
> and aware of the inadequacy
> of our table, it is to that
> uninvited the guest comes.[8]

Which is immediately followed by:

> I think that maybe
> I will be a little surer
> of being a little nearer.
> That's all. Eternity
> is in the understanding
> that that little is more than enough.[9]

---

8. Thomas, *Collected Later Poems* 1988–2000, 130; "When we are weak, we are."

9. Ibid., 131; "I think that maybe."

Works Cited

Anstey, Sandra. *R. S. Thomas: Selected Prose*. Bridgend: Seren, 1995.

Auden, W. H. *Selected Poems*. New York: Vintage, 2007.

Baudelaire, Charles. *The Flowers of Evil*. Translated by James McGowan. Oxford: Oxford University Press, 1993.

Bonhoeffer, Dietrich. *Prisoner for God: Letters and Papers from Prison*. New York: Macmillan, 1957.

Brown, Tony. *R. S. Thomas*. Cardiff: University of Wales Press, 2006.

Clark, Kenneth. *Civilisation: A Personal View*. New York: Harper & Row, 1970.

Davies, Jason Walford. *R. S. Thomas: Letters to Raymond Garlick 1951–1999*. Llandysul: Gomer, 2009.

DeWitt, Lloyd. *Rembrandt and the Face of Jesus*. Philadelphia: Philadelphia Museum of Art, 2011.

Gardner, W. H., and N. H. MacKenzie. *The Poems of Gerard Manley Hopkins*. Oxford: Oxford University Press, 1970.

Michalson, Carl. *Christianity and the Existentialists*. New York: Scribner's, 1956.

Oe, Kenzaburo. *Somersault*. Translated by Philip Gabriel. New York: Grove, 2003.

Outler, Albert C. *The Works of John Wesley*. Vol. 4, *Sermons IV*. Nashville: Abingdon, 1987.

Rogers, Byron. *The Man Who Went into the West: The Life of R. S. Thomas*. London: Aurum, 2006.

Tennant, Frederick Robert. *Philosophical Theology*. 2 vols. Cambridge: Cambridge University Press, 1928–30.

Thomas, Edward. *Collected Poems*. London: Faber, 1974.

Thomas, R. S. *Autobiographies: Former Paths; The Creative Writer's Suicide; No-One; A Year in Llŷn*. Translated by Jason Walford Davies. London: Dent, 1997.

———. *Collected Poems 1945–1990*. London: Dent, 1993.

———. *Collected Later Poems 1988–2000*. Tarset: Bloodaxe Books, 2004.

———. *The Penguin Book of Religious Verse*. Baltimore: Penguin, 1963.

———. *Poems of R. S. Thomas*. Fayetteville: University of Arkansas Press, 1985.

Tillich, Paul. *Theology of Culture*. New York: Oxford University Press, 1959.

Unamuno, Miguel de. *Tragic Sense of Life*. Translated by J. E. Crawford Flitch. New York: Dover, 1954.

Select R. S. Thomas Bibliography

R. S. Thomas: Poetry

Thomas, R. S. *Collected Poems 1945–1990*. London: Dent, 1993.
————. *Collected Later Poems 1988–2000*. Tarset: Bloodaxe Books, 2004.
————. *Poems of R. S. Thomas*. Fayetteville: University of Arkansas Press, 1985.
————. *Selected Poems*. London: Penguin, 2003

R. S. Thomas: Prose

Anstey, Sandra. *R. S. Thomas: Selected Prose*. Bridgend: Seren, 1995.
Davies, Jason Walford. *R. S. Thomas: Letters to Raymond Garlick 1951–1999*. Llandysul: Gomer, 2009.
Thomas, R. S. *Autobiographies: Former Paths; The Creative Writer's Suicide; No-One; A Year in Llŷn*. Translated by Jason Walford Davies. London: Dent, 1997.

R. S. Thomas: Biographical and Critical Studies

Brown, Tony. *R. S. Thomas*. Cardiff: University of Wales Press, 2006.
McEllhenney, John G. "'My World Stock Fluctuates a Good Deal!' An Appreciation of R. S. Thomas from the Western Side of the Atlantic." *New Welsh Review* (Summer 2002) 21–28.
————. "R. S. Thomas: Poet for Turn-of-Millennium Believers." *Quarterly Review* (Fall 1999) 267–92.
McGill, William J. *Poets' Meeting: George Herbert, R. S. Thomas, and the Argument with God*. Jefferson: McFarland, 2004.
Merchant, W. Moelwyn. *R. S. Thomas*. Fayetteville: University of Arkansas Press, 1990.
Morgan, Barry. *Strangely Orthodox: R. S. Thomas and his Poetry of Faith*. Llandysul: Gomer, 2006.
Morgan, Christopher. *R. S. Thomas: Identity, Environment, and Deity*. Manchester: Manchester University Press, 2003.
Phillips, D. Z. *R. S. Thomas: Poet of the Hidden God*. London: Macmillan, 1986.
Rogers, Byron. *The Man Who Went into the West: The Life of R. S. Thomas*. London: Aurum, 2006.

Shepherd, Elaine. *R. S. Thomas: Conceding an Absence: Images of God Explored.* New York: St. Martin's, 1996.

Ward, John Powell. *The Poetry of R. S. Thomas.* Bridgend: Seren, 2001.

Westover, Daniel. *R. S. Thomas: A Stylistic Biography.* Cardiff: University of Wales Press, 2011.

Wintle, Justin. *Furious Interiors: Wales, R. S. Thomas and God.* London: HarperCollins, 1996.

R. S. Thomas: Archives

R. S. Thomas Collection, Drew University Special Collections, Madison, NJ. Catalog online: https://uknow.drew.edu/confluence/display/Library/R.S.+Thomas+Collection

Index of the Poems
of R. S. Thomas
Quoted in This Book

Titles of poems are in *italics*; first lines are in quotes.